# REAL
# LEAN

---

## The Keys to Sustaining
## Lean Management

---

### Bob Emiliani

### Volume Three

The Center for Lean Business Management, LLC
Wethersfield, Connecticut

The Center for Lean Business Management, LLC
Wethersfield, CT
Tel: 860.558.7367    www.theclbm.com

Cover design and page layout by Tom Bittel, bittelworks@sbcglobal.net
www.dadsnoisybasement.com

Library of Congress Control Number:   2008900566
Emiliani, M.L., 1958-

**REAL LEAN: The Keys to Sustaining Lean Management (Volume Three) / M.L. Emiliani**

Includes bibliographical references and index
1. Business  2. Lean management  3. Leadership

I. Title
ISBN-13:   978-0-9722591-6-3


First Edition     June 2008

ORDERING INFORMATION
www.theclbm.com

Made in the U.S.A. using digital print-on-demand technology.

To my teachers
O.T. – D.Y. – W.J. – E.M.
and to my students.

"Our way of thinking is very difficult to copy
or even to understand."

- Fujio Cho, Chairman, Toyota Motor Corporation

# *Preface*

There is a tendency when promoting something vigorously to emphasize its positive points and minimize, or avoid entirely, any discussion of the negatives points. We see this a lot in the world of Lean management, where Lean advocates or company executives claim to have accomplished much, typically in a short period of time, but have actually accomplished very little. This is obviously self-serving for Lean advocates because it helps them generate additional interest in Lean management. It also satisfies a persistent desire in most organizations to hide behind a façade that "everything is going great." Those undergoing Lean transformations are no exception.

Unfortunately, emphasizing positives and avoiding negatives is deceptive and harmful. It can lead people to believe that adopting Lean principles and practices is easier to do than it really is. Thus, some executives will sign up for Lean management without full awareness of what they are getting into and the physical and intellectual demands that will be placed upon them if they hope to have some success.

I believe it is of the utmost importance to see things as they actually are and to convey the facts no matter how displeasing or upsetting they may be. If this is done, then people can respond to the facts, make better decisions, and hopefully find ways to improve. It is with this in mind that I paint an unvarnished picture of the reality and facts surrounding Lean management in this and the other books that I have written [1]. It is my hope, that, rather than discouraging people, the facts laid bare will motivate and inspire those who are truly committed to improving the practice of management.

Several chapters in Volume Two of *REAL LEAN* describe the important struggles that the proponents of an earlier system of industrial management, Scientific Management, faced from 1900 to the 1940s [2]. Their efforts are noteworthy because it is the closest analogue that we have to help us understand how to advance Lean management in organizations both large and small. Their failures are worth learning from because they will help us avoid repeating the same mistakes and give a clearer view of the challenges that lay before us.

Unfortunately, the proponents of Frederick W. Taylor's Scientific Management system [3] failed in their efforts to gain widespread acceptance, and the same is happening to the Lean management system today. The leading industrial and academic proponents of Scientific Management were unsuccessful in their decades-long efforts to displace less efficient and less effective conventional management practice. Harlow Person, the long-serving president of the Taylor Society, made a stunning admission in 1947 [4]:

> "In the course of his testimony before the House committee [in 1912 to Investigate the Taylor and Other Systems of Shop Management], Taylor was asked how many concerns [companies] used his system in its entirety. His reply was: 'In its entirety– none; not one.' Then, in response to another question he went on to say that a great many used it substantially, to a greater or less degree. Were Mr. Taylor alive to respond to the same question in 1947 – thirty-five years later – his reply would have to be essentially the same."

As the first generation leaders of the Scientific Management movement passed away, the second and especially the third generation leaders had different views and allowed changes in the thinking and practice of the management system to emerge. Ultimately, by the end of World War II, specific tools and practices that improved efficiency and reduced costs were separated from the Scientific Management system and subsumed into general management practice. This has already happened with Lean tools and practices such as 5S and value stream mapping, for example.

Lean management is a direct descendent of the Scientific Management system and Henry Ford's flow production system [5]. It runs the very real risk of having the same things happen to it that happened to Scientific Management and Ford's flow production system a century earlier. We have the same two problems that the leaders of the Scientific Management movement had:

1) Getting executives to understand and practice the new management system.
2) Helping them sustain its practice over generations of future managers.

Since the late 1970s the Lean management system has been terribly mischaracterized as a "manufacturing thing" and as "tools for manager's tool kit." It will be very difficult to reverse these two perceptions, though limited efforts have finally begun in 2007 [6]. Scientific Management was also mischaracterized as a "manufacturing thing" and as "tools for manager's tool kit." About 30 years were invested into advancing Scientific Management before the alarm bells went off, when its leading advocates realized there was little to show for all their effort. The exact same thing is happening today among Lean management's leaders; the alarm bells have gone off.

In addition, most of the strategies and tactics in use today to advance Lean management are largely the same as those used by Scientific Management system advocates in the early 1900s (described in Chapter 7). To be sure there are some important differences, but it is difficult to say if any will initiate a tipping point for Lean management [7], or if they will be inconsequential. Despite, or, indeed, because of this ominous picture, it is important that you proceed forward and carefully read this book. It will help you gain a thorough understanding of the issues and what you can do to address them.

While many excellent authors have focused on helping executives understand and practice the Lean management system [8], much less has been written on how to sustain its practice over generations of future managers [9]. Assuming we can get more executives to understand and practice the new management system, we must then be prepared to help them with the inevitable challenges associated with how to sustain it.

Volume Three of *REAL LEAN* is devoted to the issue of the sustainability of the Lean management system. Along the way, it also provides a significant amount of new information to executives that will help them better understand and practice the Lean management system.

Throughout this book I will often speak in general terms. I will characterize executives in certain general ways, often quite sharply, but recognizing that there are many exceptions. Please do not be put-off by some of the characterizations. Lean is a top-down management system, so there is no choice but to focus attention on those at the top. In taking this view, I do not discount the importance of mid-level managers and supervisors in helping to achieve Lean transformations.

In doing this, my intent is not to blame or disparage any individual or class of people. Instead it is to help people better understand the long-standing sustainability problem in Lean management so that better outcomes can be realized for companies and their customers. I make sincere efforts to be fact-based and simply show the many inter-related facts of Lean management that any executive schooled in conventional management would struggle to understand.

It is natural for people to want complete answers to questions such as: "How do you make Lean management stick?" However, nobody has all the answers to this important question, including me. But I can offer many new answers. Some of the answers you may like, and others you may find jarring because they threaten long-held beliefs, knowledge, or perceptions. However, I believe that upon reflection you will recognize that the information contained in this book is on-target, and that it offers substantial help to executives who are concerned about sustainability.

You must participate in the process of understanding how to sustain Lean management by gathering more information, observing, trying new things, reflecting, and thinking for yourself. Understanding the root causes of problems and identifying practical countermeasures is your job as well as mine. This

is an aspect of mutual trust and mutual respect that is necessary in order to understand problems and make improvements.

Finally, I hope you will find this book contains practical information that will help you in your efforts to comprehend and
put into practice REAL LEAN to better satisfy customers.


Bob Emiliani
2 June 2008
Wethersfield, Conn.

# *Contents*

| | | |
|---|---|---|
| Preface | | v |
| Prologue | | 1 |
| Introduction | | 9 |
| 1 | The Long-Wave Current State | 19 |
| 2 | Shortcuts to Wealth | 29 |
| 3 | Problems, Conflicts, and Costs | 37 |
| 4 | Diving to the Bottom | 49 |
| 5 | Sharing is Fundamental | 75 |
| 6 | We Need Good Students | 83 |
| 7 | Sustaining the Lean Management Movement | 89 |
| 8 | Closing Thoughts | 95 |
| Endnotes | | 101 |
| Appendix I – The Equally Important "Respect for People" Principle | | 121 |
| Appendix II – Caux Round Table *Principles for Business* | | 139 |
| About the Author | | 148 |
| Index | | 151 |

## *Prologue*

This section presents various definitions related to Lean management. The purpose is to ensure that we share a common understanding of key terms.

The *Lean management system* is defined as:

> A non-zero-sum principle-based management system focused on creating value for end-use customers and eliminating waste, unevenness, and unreasonableness using the scientific method.

In *non-zero-sum* business activities, all parties share in the gains (or losses); the so-called win-win. In contrast, *zero-sum* business activities are when one party gains at the expense of others (win-lose). Zero-sum is much more commonly found in business than non-zero-sum despite the fact that it undercuts organizational capability-building and reduces long-term competitiveness.

Zero-sum activities in business are shortcuts, where *shortcut* is defined as [1]:

> "A more direct route than the customary one, or a means of saving time or effort."

The definition of *business* is [2]:

> "Commercial, industrial, or professional dealings."

Notice that business is not formally defined as zero-sum. It is managers and executives who make business zero-sum [3].

The word *system* in the above definition of Lean management means:

> An organized and consistent set of
> principles and practices.

The Lean management system has two key principles [4]:

> "Continuous Improvement"
> and
> "Respect for People"

Where "people" means the *stakeholders* in a narrow context, and also humanity in a larger context [5]. The term *stakeholders* identifies the five key groups of people that have long-term interests in an organization's success:

> Employees, suppliers, customers,
> investors, and communities.

Competitors can be important stakeholders as well.

I will refer to the application of both the "Continuous Improvement" and "Respect for People" principles as REAL LEAN. FAKE Lean means only the "Continuous Improvement" principle is put into practice by management.

FAKE Lean retains the principal characteristics of batch-and-queue processing. We will define *batch-and-queue* as:

"A method of producing goods or services in which large batches of work are processed which sit idle in queues for long periods of time between processing steps."

I define *leadership* as [6]:

Beliefs, behaviors, and competencies that demonstrate respect for people, motivate people, improve business conditions, minimize or eliminate organizational politics, ensure effective utilization of resources, and eliminate confusion and rework.

*Waste* is defined as [7]:

"Any activity that consumes resources but creates no value for the customer."

In Lean management, the word *value* means [8]:

"The inherent worth of a product as judged by the customer and reflected in its selling price and market demand."

Its meaning should not be confused with the word "value" when used in the context of financial terms such as "shareholder value," "enterprise value," "value investing," etc.

*Unevenness* is defined as [6]:

"Work activities, information, or leadership behaviors that fluctuate significantly."

*Unreasonableness* is defined as [6]:

"Overburdening people or equipment."

Lean management recognizes eight types of waste [9, 10]:

1. Defects
2. Transportation
3. Overproduction
4. Waiting
5. Processing
6. Movement
7. Inventory
8. Behaviors

The context for the eighth waste is leadership behaviors.

Chapter 4 includes discussion related to value stream maps. Readers should be familiar with how to interpret these diagrams [11].

The Japanese word "kaizen" means:

"Change for the better"
*in a multilateral context.*

Kaizen is a process for making small improvements on a daily basis. It is preferable to participate in kaizen because infrequent, large step-function changes are much more difficult for people to achieve.

We will refer to *buyers' markets* and *sellers' markets*. These terms are defined as follows:

A buyers' market is a competitive marketplace where many companies (sellers) exist to satisfy customers' (buyers') wants and needs. This type of market typically favors buyers' interests.

A sellers' market is a non-competitive marketplace where one or two companies (sellers) exist to satisfy customers' (buyers') wants and needs. This type of market typically favors sellers' interests.

Executives can be ignorant of these markets or they can confuse these two markets and be seller-focused when they should be customer-focused.

We will understand Lean to be a top-down management system, and where buy-in among all members of the senior management team is required.

The framework for comprehending the position of executives, the officers of the company, includes the following:

- They are in charge of the organization.
- They may or may not be leaders.
- They have planning, organizing, coordination, and control functions.
- They have authority to change the management system, policies, practices, procedures, and business performance metrics.
- They have authority to ensure conformance.
- They are responsible for organizational successes and failures.

- They receive the most compensation.

Executives are the highest level of authority in an organization, which means "the buck stops" with them: They make the decisions that lead to the success or failure of Lean transformations. They are ultimately responsible for their decisions, positive outcomes as well as negative outcomes, and for both intended and unintended consequences.

We will assume that boards of directors generally support executives' business proposals and strategic direction, and that executives try to do good work.

Executives, like anyone, often make incorrect assumptions or have incomplete, flawed, or mistaken views, knowledge, or information and therefore can make many wrong decisions.

We will recognize executives as actors in processes to satisfy customers' wants and needs, and that the processes contain many types of defects whose causes come from many different sources. Thus, executives are responsible for poor outcomes [12]. But are they to blame? Certainly not, if they accept fault for their errors, and then strive to identify root causes and implement practical countermeasures.

Lastly, readers will periodically come across the following symbol and words:

   Executive decision point for sustaining
                       Lean management.

This indicates a decision that executives have to make. If they say "yes," then they are indicating their intent to commit to that particular decision point.

Saying "yes" to all 14 decision points, and keeping these commitments, will greatly improve the chance of sustaining the Lean management system.

# *Introduction*

This volume of *REAL LEAN* focuses sustainability from two perspectives:

- Sustaining the Lean management system within an organization
- Sustaining the Lean management movement

Much greater emphasis will be placed on sustaining Lean within an organization – REAL LEAN, where both principles, "Continuous Improvement" and "Respect for People," are practiced [1] (see Appendix I). This book is not concerned with sustaining FAKE Lean, where only the "Continuous Improvement" principle is practiced [2, 3].

There will also be some important thoughts on how to sustain the Lean management movement in light of the many systems, methods, practices, tools, etc., that Lean management competes against. This is something that deeply concerns the leaders of the Lean movement.

The question that has long been asked by almost every Lean practitioner is: "How do you make Lean stick?" There is a consuming interest in this question, and the answer given is to create a Lean culture [4] or correct the broad-based confusion that exists in companies over priorities and responsibilities [5].

We know from The Wiremold Company's story that a Lean culture was created between 1991 and 2001, but it did not stick [6]. The culture changed soon after new owners completed the installation of a management team who knew little about Lean. CEOs say to me: "But what about all the other employees who learned Lean? I can't believe they couldn't keep it going." Believe it. There is much more to sustainability than creating a Lean culture, as is commonly understood, or clarifying priorities and responsibilities.

To most people, Toyota Motor Corporation epitomizes a Lean culture [7]. They think Toyota will be Lean no matter what happens because it is in their DNA. However, Toyota executives are constantly worried about complacency and backslide [8], which indicates that they too have deep concerns about sustainability. Careful observation of Toyota executives' actions reveals a steady stream of countermeasures designed to help perpetuate and improve their management system.

Toyota executives know from experience that their management system does not automatically sustain itself [9]. The DNA of the Toyota Way is not encoded into people in the same way as human deoxyribonucleic acid is encoded into people. It is a poor comparison; one that confuses rather than clarifies. The former lies at the surface and can be quite easily pushed aside or disabled – as history has shown time and time again [10] – while human DNA is deeply embedded and is much more difficult to change.

People's search for sustainability operates under the assumption that Lean management is sustainable. However, referring to Lean as a "journey" means we never get to the final destination, which implies that sustainability is elusive, and likely never attainable. Similarly, the phrase "continuous improvement" implies that we are never done improving, and that we always have more to learn about Lean management itself, as well as our customers, our suppliers, our business processes, etc.

Let's take a simple analogy. If you hold a ball up in the air, at what point can you let it go and have it remain in the air by itself? The answer is never, as long as the earth has gravity. Likewise, conventional management is like the earth's gravity; it is a strong, constant force upon Lean people to return to conventional ways of thinking and doing things. It is not reasonable to hope that Lean someday will automatically stick by itself. Lean requires constant inputs of resources to counter the force of conventional management gravity.

The question is: What can you do to manage gravity and reduce the odds of backslide? That is what this book is about. You will learn that Lean is a much bigger challenge than you previously thought, and to enjoy some success you will have to think differently to a much greater extent than you have anticipated.

Continuing with the ball analogy; if you toss it into the air, it will fall back to Earth due to gravity. But as you know, the situation is not hopeless. You can apply more energy (and technology) and launch a ball into orbit. However, it will be stuck in an elliptical trajectory that will decay and eventually cause the ball to fall back to Earth. You can apply even more energy and escape Earth's gravity at high speed via parabolic or hyperbolic trajectories.

FAKE Lean is like tossing a ball up into the air and falling back to Earth, whereas REAL LEAN is like launching a ball into Earth orbit. However, various features of conventional thinking are embedded in conventional management, which this book highlights, and act as forces which cause the orbit to decay. These forces include: power, control, local optimization, zero-sum, results focus, batch-and-queue processing, ignorance, selfishness, and most common business metrics. It is not possible to completely escape conventional management's gravity. The best we can hope to do is manage it and try to stay in orbit for a long time.

So how can an organization increase its probability of sustaining and improving its Lean management practice? How can an organization reduce the burdens associated with sustainability over generations of managers? Let's start by examining the easy stuff and getting that out of the way, in preparation for more detailed analyses in subsequent chapters.

History shows us that senior managers have great difficulty trying to implement and sustain a new management system and make many unforced errors [11]. Figure 1 lists seven items that we know with great certainly will happen to any business, and which will greatly reduce the probability of sustaining Lean management.

### Figure 1 – Business Certainties

- Company ownership will change — 99% chance
- Executives will change — 100% chance
- Executives will misunderstand Lean — 99% chance
- Executives will misapply Lean
  - Principles — 99% chance
  - Practices — 90% chance
- Will not change accounting system — 99% chance
- Will not budget for Lean to achieve desired outcomes — 75% chance
- Executive will not participate — 99% chance

**Certainty #1 – Company Ownership Will Change**
Companies are bought and sold every day, in hostile or friendly takeovers, etc. When this happens, new managers are brought in. Invariably, the new managers know little or nothing about Lean management. Within a few years they will undo almost all Lean thinking and practice and return the business to conventional management [12].

**Certainty #2 – Executives Will Change**
Without any change in ownership, there will of course be turnover in the executive ranks every few years. The new executives usually know nothing about Lean. In addition, they will favor different practices that they learned in previous assignments or at other companies, which often conflict with Lean management. They will seek to minimize or dismantle Lean thinking and practice in their department or functional area of responsibility. A new CEO or president can quickly reverse Lean company-wide.

At the surface level, changes in company ownership and changes in senior management account for the vast majority of cases where companies were unable to sustain Lean practice (and Scientific Management before that). Subsequent chapters will reveal what's going on below the surface.

**Certainty #3 – Executives Will Misunderstand Lean**
The vast majority of executives will misunderstand Lean management. They will try to fit Lean into their current knowledge and understanding of conventional management practice. In doing so, they will invariably discard the key elements of Lean management that make it work. This was true back in the days of Scientific Management as well.

**Certainty #4 – Executives Will Misapply Lean**
Executives cannot apply Lean correctly if they don't understand it. Some will deliberately implement FAKE Lean to obtain short-term gains. This approach has long been favored, going back to the days of Scientific Management, because Lean affects senior managers – and that's bad. It places great demands upon them. Most senior managers do not want to be affected by Lean management, but they don't mind if other people are affected. That, of course, is inconsistent with the "Respect for People" principle. They end up verbally supporting the deployment of Lean tools and don't do much else.

To be sure, in some cases executives have no ill intentions and are just not familiar with REAL LEAN. But most, it seems, fail to go find out what REAL LEAN is, and so they commit an unforced error. The effect is the same as deliberately implementing FAKE Lean for short-term gains.

**Certainty #5 – Executives Will Not Change the Accounting System**
Large companies invest millions of dollars in their accounting software systems, which are typically rooted in calculations that are inconsistent with Lean principles and practices such as: economic order quantities, quantity discount analysis, standard costs, earned hours, purchase price variance, etc. The sunk cost, in dollars, is huge, and acts as a deterrent to implementing Lean accounting and using metrics that are consistent with Lean principles and practices.

But there is another sunk cost: knowledge, which also acts as a deterrent to improvement. Changing the accounting system to reflect Lean processes requires the CEO, CFO, and others to unlearn, re-learn, and recognize limitations and deficiencies in their working knowledge of accounting and their accounting education. Most CFOs don't want to do that. They'll say their job is hard enough without having to learn Lean accounting [13]. An accounting system and metrics that support conventional management practices will obviously make it impossible to enjoy success with Lean management, let alone sustain it.

**Certainty #6 – Executives Will Not Budget for Lean**
Lean costs some money to implement and sustain, but not a lot of money if you do it right. Typically, companies either don't budget for Lean activities, or they allocate budget for Lean activities to each department. In the former, most people know if there is no budget, it's not real. Employees know management expects something for nothing, and the something they get is almost nothing. In the latter case, operating cost overruns incurred by departments will usually be covered by the budget intended for Lean activities. This serves as a disincentive to do Lean – in part because the budgeting process if full of waste and errors, which lead to budgets that virtually guarantee operating cost overruns.

**Certainty #7 – Executives Will Not Participate in Lean**
Most senior managers don't participate in Lean because they think they are "beyond that," feel they do not have anything new to learn, or that Lean offers no new learning opportunities. Many also see it as time taken away from internal politicking or obsequious behaviors. They are afraid of looking stupid or making mistakes, which they feel would compromise their leadership. Whatever the reason, it is very difficult to get executives to participate in improvement activities once

in a while, let alone on a consistent basis.

These are the first seven strikes against sustaining Lean; that's a lot of strikes. It's no wonder why so few companies have had much Lean success to begin with, let alone sustain it beyond one generation of executives.

In contrast, look at what the executives of Toyota Motor Corporation do – or what any management team should do – to make these seven certainties much less certain:

- They do things to avoid disruptive changes in ownership.
- They train new executives in Toyota's management system [14].
- They make sure new executives do not misunderstand Toyota's management system.
- They make sure new executives do not misapply Toyota Way principles and practices.
- While the accounting system may be fairly conventional, they are not ruled by it in the same way that conventionally-managed business are ruled by it. Toyota managers recognize the flaws in standard (absorption) cost accounting and take into account other types of information and time-based metrics.
- They allocate budget for improvement activities (as well as being part of everyone's daily job) and training.
- All executives participate in improvement activities.

Toyota executives are not perfect. They make mistakes and the company has backslid at times in the past [15], and you can expect them to do so at times in the future. Toyota executives recognize this better than anyone, and so they continuously develop and implement countermeasures to increase the probability of sustaining and improving their management practice over generations of future managers. Their culture has to be maintained and further developed by every employee every day. If not, it will backslide towards conventional management.

You can do the same things that Toyota executives do to lessen the effects of the seven certainties, and more, if you give some thought to Lean enterprise estate planning [16].

We have examined the easy stuff. Let's begin a more detailed analysis of the challenge of sustaining and improving the Lean management system. In order to do this, we have to think about this problem from different perspectives and go well beyond the obvious explanations. Failure to do so will ensure we remain mired in the long-wave current state.

# 1 The Long-Wave Current State

The term *long-wave current state* is used here to describe a current state that has existed over a long period of time. It helps put the many challenges of Lean management into a broader historical context.

The first challenge in Lean management is to gain executive buy-in. Lean is not a bottom-up management system; it is top-down. If senior managers are not interested in Lean management, then the company does not adopt Lean management. Executives will pursue different strategies and directions, and employees will follow management's lead even if it is crazy and results in many new or recurring problems.

Historically, since the time of Scientific Management system and Ford's flow production system to present-day Lean management, it has been very difficult to obtain executive buy-in. Typically the president or CEO wants to improve profitability or suddenly, unexpectedly, faces cost problems. They will normally seek simple solutions and immediate results. To achieve this, they will hire consultants who can achieve what the boss wants, usually with little or no concern for employees who may lose their job or others who might be negatively impacted. Seventy-five years ago, these types of consultants were referred to disparagingly as "Bedaux consultants," named after Charles Bedaux (1886-1944) [1], a prominent industrial management consultant.

Charles Bedaux, and other consultants like him, focused narrowly on one thing: saving their client money. Consultants offering this narrow promise have been much more success-ful than those who proposed broad, fundamental changes to the management system to achieve both short- and long-term benefits. In fact, the originators of the Scientific Management system were far less successful in their consulting than were the consultants who cherry-picked the system and applied the tools that offered the quickest cost savings and efficiency improvements. Needless to say, the originators of the management system had great disdain for "Bedaux consultants," but not because they were jealous of their success. It was because they were corrupting and misusing the Scientific Management system, knew that employees would suffer, and that the company's gains would be short-lived.

Sure enough, the client company improved its operations and its profitability for a while, but would soon face another cycle of distress. Most top managements since the 1890s seem quite content to face a crisis, fix it, face another crisis, fix it, face another crisis, fix it, and so on. This implies that there is virtually no interest among executives for fundamental changes in management practice. In other words, there is no real marketplace demand for a new management system. But there is plenty of marketplace demand for quick fixes. Hence the great success of the "Bedaux consultants."

As you might expect, some company presidents wanted to escape the cycle of distress and make fundamental improvements to the management system. So what did they do? In the early 1900s they would contact the creators of Scientific Management or the head of The Taylor Society and ask for assistance. The advice given consisted of three items:

- Read the books and papers on Scientific Management
- Go see examples of companies using Scientific Management
- Start practicing Scientific Management in your own company

There was an expectation among the leaders of the Scientific Management movement that company presidents would personally engage in some heavy lifting; that they would study the system by reading books and papers on the topic, that they would observe the system in action at different companies, and that they would endure the challenge of practicing Scientific Management in their own company. Presidents were expected to think and participate in the installation of the Scientific Management system, not delegate it to others.

However, once presidents got to know more about Scientific Management, the less they liked it. That's because the management system places great physical and intellectual demands on presidents [2], as well as all other managers and supervisors. Company presidents did not want to make a commitment in their time and energy, and they did not want their managers to revolt. But they did see the merits in improving efficiency and reducing costs, so they took the easy way out – a shortcut. They outsourced the task to "Bedaux consultants" and delegated their responsibilities to a supervisor who was reassigned to become an improvement leader. This is a strategy commonly used by presidents to reduce risk and errors, at least from their point of view.

So what do we do today to try and gain buy-in among senior managers? We do things that are very similar to what was done in the early 1900s:

- Give executives books to read
- Provide examples of success stories in their industry
- Arrange tours of Lean companies
- Train executives in the basics of Lean
  (usually just the tools)
- Do pilot projects to demonstrate the benefits

But even after doing these things, we still face resistance from executives. Why? As I said earlier, there is virtually no marketplace demand for a new management system. But there is demand for tools that can be used on a narrow utilitarian basis to satisfy short-term needs, usually applied in a zero-sum fashion (where one party gains at the expense of others). This distorts and corrupts the management system to the point where it is hardly recognizable. This outcome greatly upset the creators of Scientific Management because "Bedaux consultants" claimed to be disciples of Scientific Management, but actually knew very little about it. The same thing happens today with Lean management.

This outcome leads next to an examination of the short-term focus possessed by most senior managers. First, let's answer the question: Where do company presidents and CEOs come from? The usual path is they start at or near the bottom of the company. They are hourly or salaried workers whose focus is to deal with short-term problems. If they do a good job they get promoted to supervisor where they still deal with short-term problems.

If they succeed with that, they get promoted to the manager

level. But do they now start to distance themselves from short-term problems and deal with mid-term problems? Usually no. If they are good at fighting fires as a manager, they often get promoted to executive level [3]. By this time, they will have spent 15-25 years focused on the short-term, and applying many shortcuts to help them achieve short-term results along the way (e.g. workarounds). It should be no surprise that they continue to do what they are most familiar with doing: dealing with short-term problems. Every now and then they will need help dealing with short-term problems, so they will call in the very successful "Bedaux consultants."

This leads to a conundrum: How do we reconcile top executive's desire for "world-class" company performance when their focus on the short-term is deeply embedded and they have a constant desire to take shortcuts? It could be that they don't know what "world-class" is. Or, it could be that they don't think their short-term focus is harmful. After all, look how they succeeded, and "it's just the nature of business," they might say. It could also be that they don't think they are taking shortcuts.

By way of comparison, can world-class athletes or top musicians have a short-term focus and take shortcuts. The answer is no, assuming they are not cheating – steroids for athletes or fake singing or playing by musicians. You must possess a long-term view to become world-class, without losing sight of short- and mid-term time-frames, and you can't take shortcuts.

Henry Gantt was a contemporary of Frederick Taylor and one of his disciples. He spent decades interacting with executives and had these sharp words to say about them in 1919, near the end of his life [3]:

> "In attempting to rate the influence of executives on production we must recognize the fact that under our present methods executives as a rule seem to favor that system of production which to the greatest extent possible relieves them of responsibility.
>
> ..there is a tendency to blame the man lower down, rather than the man higher up with the result that the man in the shop may be reprimanded, or even discharged, for an error in judgment which caused the loss of a few dollars, while the man at the top making a similar error in judgment costing thousands of dollars, too frequently gets by without anybody's knowing that the loss was due to his failure.
>
> It is not claimed that executives in general desire to shirk their responsibility and place the blame on others, but our business methods are still dominated by the spirit of the past, which was 'the king can do no wrong,' that is to say... 'he has a right to do it.'"

Gantt is lamenting the fact that executives typically take shortcuts, make errors, and then proclaim no error has been made. Thus, the king can do no wrong. Is the spirit of the past still with us today? It seems to be, but how do we know for sure?

We know it by understanding how executives perceived Scientific Management in the past and how they perceive the Lean management system today. To them it is OK to distort and corrupt the management system to suit one's own needs.

Low fidelity versions of Lean management are good enough, so, too, must be any associated shortcuts that are taken to achieve this. Executives' perception of Lean management is correct no matter what it is. This is not theory. It has been the case throughout the history of modern management practice. We see the reality of this in the myriad flavors of Lean management that exist today.

It is a big problem if any version of the Lean management system can be the right version. Thankfully that does not mean no version of Lean is the right version. There is a right version of Lean management, just as there was a right version of Scientific Management, when it comes to the fundamental principles, practices, and tools.

The fact that executives' perception of Lean management is correct no matter what version of Lean it is suggests that leaders are being self-serving, which is an aspect of zero-sum thinking.

 Executive decision point #1 for sustaining Lean management:

> Lean management requires leaders to
> serve others, not themselves. Self-serving
> leadership is a shortcut. Can you commit
> to servant leadership? Yes or no?

Gantt's condemnation of executives as "kings who can do no wrong" has one other very important ramification: that of "knowing it all."

Professional workers often receive scholarly journals published by the societies to which they are members. My father was a scientist who subscribed to the primary journals in his field, and he dutifully kept up with the literature throughout his professional career. When I was a metallurgist I could not wait for the next issue or *Metallurgical Transactions A* and *Acta Metallurgica*. You hope that your primary care physician is keeping up with each issue of *Journal of the American Medical Association*.

What we know about executives is that most don't read books and journals, and if they do it is usually not about business [4]. Since, according to Gantt, they can do no wrong, the possibility of repeating the errors made by other executives is irrelevant to them. So why bother spending the time to read business books and management journals and periodicals that report on or analyze these errors? Instead they staunchly defend themselves when they have made errors and shift the blame to others, which is zero-sum thinking.

You would hope that the president of your company is keeping up with the management literature well enough to learn from the daily avalanche of errors made by executives in other companies and figure out the root causes and countermeasures to avoid those same errors from happening to your company [5]. However, that does not seem to happen, which indicates executives don't believe they have much to learn. Therefore, they must think they know it all.

Executive decision point #2 for sustaining
Lean management:

> Lean management requires leaders who can admit
> they don't know it all. Thinking you know it all is
> a shortcut. Can you admit you don't know it all to
> yourself and others? Yes or no?

How can it be that executives think they know it all (and, relatedly, control it all)? This seems like a vexing question, but there is actually a very simple answer. It turns out it is easy to think you can know it all by having a zero-sum (win-lose) view of business. That's all it takes. In mathematics, this is called a *determinate equation*; an equation with a unique solution.

Conversely, it is impossible to know it all if you have non-zero-sum view of business. In mathematics, this is called an *indeterminate equation*; an equation with many solutions or approximations.

According to Katsuaki Watanabe, the president of Toyota Motor Corporation [6]:

> "There's no end to the process of learning about
> the Toyota Way. I don't think I have a complete
> understanding even today, and I have worked for
> the company for 43 years."

A distinctive feature of The Toyota Way [7] is that it is a non-zero-sum management system. So according to Watanabe, it is impossible to have a complete understanding of a non-zero-sum management system. He should know.

Lean management requires leaders who can operate a non-zero-sum management system. That's a problem because executives are trained in school and on-the-job, over many years, to operate a zero-sum management system. As a result, conducting business in a non-zero-sum way with employees, suppliers, customers, investors, and communities is a new and unfamiliar challenge that most executives shrink from.

Executive decision point #3 for sustaining Lean management:

> Lean management requires leaders who are willing to learn how to operate a non-zero-sum management system. Can you commit to learning about non-zero-sum Lean management?
> Yes or no?

History shows that the vast majority of executives have said "no" to this decision point.

# 2 Shortcuts to Wealth

Most top executives view their role primarily in one of two ways: to create wealth – often incorrectly characterizing it as "maximize shareholder value" – or to satisfy customers. You can imagine a lot of executives say: "I do both." However, if you carefully study their decisions you find that they typically do mostly one or the other, which communicates their true intentions [1].

Perhaps 99 percent of executives feel their primary responsibility is to create wealth. Focusing on creating wealth is a winner for them in terms of public visibility and financial rewards. And, there's a big bag of tricks to draw upon to create wealth. It's pretty easy to do, as you will soon see.

On the other hand, maybe 1 or 2 percent of executives truly feel their prime responsibility is to satisfy customers. In general, there is less public visibility and less financial rewards. The bag of tricks to draw upon is tiny, and it is harder to satisfy customers than to create wealth – or the appearance of wealth (think of Enron, for example). However, if executives do a good job satisfying customers, they usually end up creating a lot of wealth.

You should notice a problem here. All executives whose companies serve competitive markets say they are customer-focused – by that they mean they are responsive to buyers' markets. That implies their duty first and foremost is to satisfy customers, but that is what only a small percentage of executives actually do. Most are shareholder-focused, despite the fact that many shareholders are gamers and gamblers who don't think or act like owners. It is wiser for executives to focus on satisfying customers, the source of cash flow, than on gamblers.

So what shortcuts do CEOs (and chief financial officers) use to create wealth? They work from a well-worn playbook, whose content broadly fits into two categories: legislative and regulatory shortcuts, and management shortcuts [2]. The legislative and regulatory category includes:

### Legislative / Regulatory Shortcuts
Ease Anti-Trust Laws
Limit Union Eligibility
Restrict Overtime Pay
Reduce Disclosure Requirements
Change Compensation Rules
Accounting Rules / Materiality
Reduce Corporate Taxes
Extend Patent Duration
Seek Trade Restrictions
Limit Minimum Wages

In this category, they will lobby Congress and state and federal regulatory agencies to obtain more favorable conditions under which to do business. Much of it relates to cost reduction or sales expansion.

The management category includes:

## Management Shortcuts

Layoffs
Cut Pay and Benefits
Reduce Influence of Labor
Close Facilities
Squeeze Suppliers
Outsource
Share Buy-Back
Acquire, Merge, or Divest Assets
Incentive Compensation
Accounting Methods
Reduce Taxes
Management Shake-Up

These are actions that executives have more direct control over and can do mostly at-will to improve financial performance. While not comprehensive lists, they illustrate an important point. That is, these are quick-hit, zero-sum tactics, where one party gains at the expense of others [3]. These shortcuts are mostly learned on-the-job, or by watching what executives in other companies do. While it is very expensive to do these things, they are, paradoxically, done to try to lower the cost of conventional management practice – which relies on expensive overproduction to compete, as you will see in Chapter 4.

Zero-sum tactics are shortcuts. Anyone can apply these shortcuts; executives do not need MBAs or even college degrees to do it. A middle school student can do these things in any order, and then repeat as necessary to achieve the desired financial objective, just as most executives do.

Shortcuts are very appealing to people. High school and college students love CliffsNotes (these days, sparknotes.com) and use them to avoid reading the book that the teacher assigned. When we struggle with math problems in school we desperately seek shortcuts to the solution. For term papers, students increase the font size, decrease the margins, and make the graphics bigger to increase the number of pages and reduce the number of words. People cheat on tests when cramming for the test (another shortcut) doesn't work out. They cheat by collaborating on individual assignments. Students try to get parents to provide answers. Kids like to take shortcuts through neighbors' yards to get home from school. And many people like to play the lottery in hopes of getting rich quick and avoid having to work hard all of our lives.

Shortcuts are plentiful in business. The boss says: "I don't care how you do it, just get it done" or "Do whatever it takes," thus encouraging workers to take shortcuts. Short-term thinking is a huge driver for taking shortcuts. We eagerly await forecasts (fortune-telling) rather than work hard to improve business processes and strengthen our abilities to quickly respond to changing market conditions. Price fixing is a shortcut, illegal of course. So is insider trading and stock option backdating – also illegal. We blame others when we have problems: employees, other managers, other departments, suppliers, customers, the weather, etc. We use metrics that are shortcuts for telling us how we are doing, such as: purchase price variance, standard costs, and earned hours.

When the business has problems, executives lay people off, close plants and offices, and squeeze suppliers for lower prices. All are shortcuts. When the business has bigger problems, there is a "management shake-up" to fix the business; a shortcut that reveals nothing about the underlying problems. And, of course, we have "economic man," the classical and neo-classical economists' view that people are rational self-interested maximizers [4]. This is the granddaddy of all shortcuts [5, 6] because it drives most other shortcuts in business. It gives executives a free pass (a "free lunch," in economic terms) to ignore all costs associated with selfishness.

Shortcuts to wealth are irresistible, especially if intellectuals say they are acceptable. A shortcut that has widespread appeal, and that a majority of people can agree on, apparently is not a shortcut at all. It becomes a tenet that legitimizes actions taken by people to be rational self-interested maximizers. However, the creation of "economic man" is a simple confirmation bias trap [7]: where people seek evidence that supports their views or desires and discard any evidence that contradicts it. It is an endless do-loop as shown in Figure 2-1, because false statements are never allowed.

**Figure 2-1**

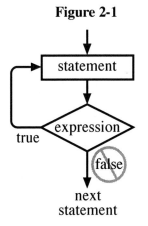

next
statement

If you overheard me saying to my wife: "I need to sell some books to make some money," you might assume that money was my driving force for writing books and that I am a rational self-interested maximizer. If so, you would have severely misjudged my motivation.

I write books to help me understand things so I can help other people understand things. It is an activity that I like to do, and it organizes and documents my thought processes and ideas. I do not expect to make money just because I wrote a book. I do expect to make money if the book sells because it satisfies market demand for such information. Making money is the financial reward for a job well done. Other rewards come from front- and back-end parts of the processes, including feedback from readers.

Many people attribute short-term thinking and the resultant shortcuts taken to pressure coming from Wall Street. However, private owners can place as much or more short-term pressure on executives [8]. So this explanation does not have much to offer. It is likely that short-term thinking is to some degree hard-wired into our brains as a mechanism to help humans survive. However, this programming does not generally serve a useful purpose in business.

Focusing on the short-term can be exhilarating and provide a strong sense of accomplishment. Working in this mode for a decade or two is powerful training that appears to be facilitated by basic human programming. However, it can be addictive and turn into an obsessive-compulsive behavior that is hard to break free from, but can indeed be done.

Executives have choices in the methods they can use to create wealth. The most common are the *á la carte*, zero-sum, closed system methods contained in the "CEO playbook" that simply transfer wealth from other parties to themselves and the company. How to create wealth from waste, as capable Lean leaders do, is not well-understood by others. It is a non-zero-sum, open system where parties share in the wealth created – not necessarily equally, but in ways that the parties judge as fair.

In essence, the Lean management system competes against other things that executives can do to create wealth and satisfy customers. Unfortunately, most executives see Lean as just another *á la carte* method at their disposal, not as a management system. Between 1990 and 2001, the enterprise value of The Wiremold Company increased 16 times, while shareholder vale increased over 6 times [9]. The reality is that you don't need Lean management to create those stunning numbers. You can do it using *á la carte*, zero-sum, closed system, shortcuts contained in the CEO playbook. Along with that, however, you are virtually guaranteed to get the face a crisis, fix it, face another crisis, fix it, face another crisis, fix it problem.

It is not likely that Lean management will ever win this competition on a broad scale. But it may do so in certain companies in several different industries. In order for that to happen, executives will need to overcome some additional barriers. One is that the people who see waste, unevenness, and unreasonableness are viewed as oddballs; the lunatic fringe; about the same as UFO hunters. They need to be seen as leaders, and whose words:

"We have almost unlimited waste, unevenness,
and unreasonableness."

make a lot more sense than those from executives who say:

"We have limited resources."

Executive decision point #4 for sustaining
Lean management:

> Lean management requires executives who
> will do the work. Can you commit to
> eliminating the shortcuts? Yes or no?

# 3 Problems, Conflict, and Costs

The key management issues for over 100 years have centered on four points: power, control, wealth, and freedom. Efforts to implement the Scientific Management system in companies always bumped up against these four issues. So, whether an owner, manager, worker, union, consultant, or politician, they all had a one problem or another with Scientific Management:

- Division of Labor
- Speeding Up Workers
- Prescribing Work Methods
- Cost Problems (higher wages)
- Loss of Authority, Control
- Sharing Power
- Dividing Surpluses
- Layoffs and Labor Market Turmoil
- Scientific Selection & Development of Workers
- Rule of Thumb and Opinion vs. Facts & Scientific Investigation
- Erratic, Fickle Management

Whether you are an owner, manager, worker, union, consultant, or politician, everyone will have a one problem or another with Lean Management, similar to the above list.

Part of the discord is driven by the narrow understanding that most executives have of problems. Figure 3-1a shows how most people see problems: as simple linear relationships.

**Figure 3-1a**

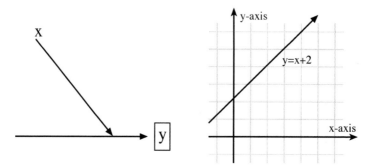

Mathematically, it is a y = f(x) world for most executives. They possess a 2-dimensional algebraic view of problems. Figure 3-1b illustrates the linear relationship between cost and volume that most executives have in mind. If you want to lower costs, you have to produce more, which is classic batch-and-queue thinking. The result of this is that executives see only part of picture, not the entire picture.

**Figure 3-1b**

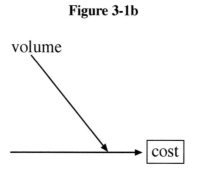

There are other liabilities that come with this way of thinking that cause organizations to under-perform. For example, many executives view their choices of actions to take as control knobs labeled: price, labor [1], material, and overhead. This persistently simplistic view results in a failure to recognize deeper inter-relationship and nuances, which of course helps the "Bedaux consultants" because they don't have to bother to recognize the deeper inter-relationship and nuances either.

Once again, this brings us back to the problem of short-term thinking and the shortcuts that are taken to achieve short-term results. Think of this analogy: In a sport such as cycling, you have different types of competitions: sprints and distance races. Each requires different equipment, training, nutrition, strength, strategy, and tactics. Executives are trained in business through 20 years of short-term projects and assignments, with short-term goals and short-term rewards. They are trained to be sprinters [2].

The problem is that Lean management is for distance competitions, not sprints. The executives who embark on a Lean transformation, and Scientific Management before that, possess skills that are the opposite of what is needed. They are almost completely unprepared for what lies ahead. You can see why making the transition is so difficult for most executives. In fact, most don't make the transition and remain stuck in the sprinters' world, which has higher costs.

How do we know for sure that the costs are higher?

Most businesses operate in the absence of explicit business principles. That's quite amazing. It is like finding a wallet in the street, and, in the absence of principles, you can decide to do any of the following:

- Keep it
- Keep the cash and return the rest
- Keep the credit cards and return the rest
- Keep the driver's license and return the rest
- Keep the family photos and return the rest
- Return it

Any of these decisions are acceptable in the absence of principles. However, what did our parents and elementary school teachers tell us to do? To take nothing and return the wallet to its owner immediately.

Did your business school professors or the supervisors you had in your first six years at work teach you business principles? Probably not; at least not explicitly. If they did, it probably would have been related to how to respond to short-term pressures and take shortcuts. These are bad principles that serve as a poor guide to personal and business conduct.

Toyota Motor Corporation has three documents that describe its business principles: The "Toyoda Precepts," "Guiding Principles at Toyota," and "Contribution Towards Sustainable Development" [3]. The role that these play in their business will be discussed in more detail later, but for now let's just say that these multilateral business principles support good personal and business conduct. These documents are extremely important to Toyota executives because there are many consequences to unprincipled business activities, some of which are severe.

There is a useful generic expression of non-zero-sum multilateral business principles that any company can adopt called the Caux Round Table *Principles for Business* [4] (see Appendix II). The *Principles for Business* is a practical, real-world description of principled business behavior crafted by CEO-level business leaders. It describes the types of relationships that business executives should want to seek with their key stakeholders – customers, employees, suppliers, investors, communities, and competitors – and consists of seven general principles and six stakeholder principles. The *Principles for Business* can help move executives away from zero-sum, short-term, shortcut-driven management thinking and practices.

Graphically, what does it look like when executives are driven by zero-sum, short-term, shortcut-driven management thinking and practices over many years? Figure 3-2 shows various categories of the Caux Round Table *Principles for Business* on a radar chart and a plot of the aggregate results from a survey of nearly 250 independent contributors, supervisors, managers, and executives regarding their perceptions of their organization's performance when benchmarked against the *Principles for Business*. The survey participants worked in for-profit businesses, not-for-profit organizations, and government agencies.

## Figure 3-2

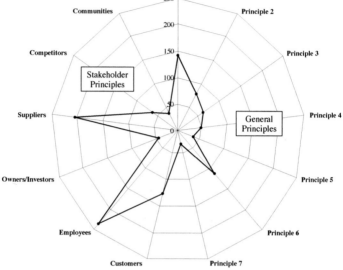

The data points that are further away from the center indicate a perception of inconsistency between their organization's performance and the *Principles for Business*. So there appears to be a lot of inconsistency: specifically with respect to Principles 1 and 6, and the "Employees," "Suppliers," and "Customers" categories. The result was remarkably similar in for-profit businesses, not-for-profit organizations, and government agencies, which indicates that zero-sum, short-term, shortcut-driven management thinking and practices are common regardless of the type of organization.

Figure 3-2 tells us that employees feel their leaders strongly marginalize their interests and those of their suppliers. It tells us that employees feel their leaders could do much more to balance the interests of other stakeholders (Principle 1) and reduce the company's environmental footprint (Principle 6). It tells us that employees feel customers could be treated better.

It also tells us that employees feel investors are being treated in a manner that is consistent with *Principles for Business*. But is this really true; are investors really being treated well? No they are not, because employees, suppliers, and customers interests are being marginalized. So the practical impact of zero-sum, short-term, shortcut-driven management thinking and practice is to drive important stakeholders away. If they feel marginalized they will work against the company in subtle and not-so-subtle ways. It drives opportunistic behaviors among those who have been marginalized. This clearly increases costs to a business, through delays, rework, quality problems, longer lead-times, and higher prices. Looking at Figure 3-2, it is not surprising that the top two areas of corporate litigation are employment (Employees) and contracts (Suppliers).

As you can imagine, management consultants love executives who are committed to high cost zero-sum, short-term, shortcut-driven management thinking and practices. There will always be steady business for them – yet another cost to the company.

To further amplify these important points, let's turn to music. What would the simplistic view of problems and the high cost zero-sum, short-term, shortcut-driven management thinking and practice that executives favor sound like if we could hear it? It would of course be a simple single-instrument tune. It would sound like the tune "chopstix" played on the piano. There is no skill in doing that. Likewise, there is no skill in possessing simplistic views of problems and zero-sum, short-term, shortcut-driven management thinking and practices.

How do Lean executives view problems? They see problems differently; in much greater detail and with much higher fidelity. Figure 3-3 shows how Lean people see problems. Not as simple linear relationships, which they can certainly see as well, but as more elaborate and detailed relationships.

**Figure 3-3**

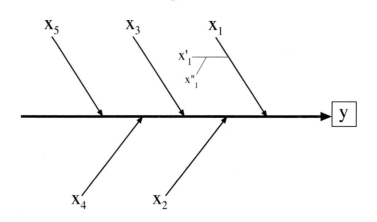

Mathematically, it is a non-linear world for Lean executives. They possess a 6-dimensional, calculus view of problems. If you want to lower costs, maybe you don't have to produce more. Instead, you have to better understand customers wants and needs, what they are willing to pay, how to achieve flow, and how to improve responsiveness to customer demand. The result of this view of problems is that Lean executives see most, if not all, of the picture. It is much more difficult to compete against that.

There are other benefits that come with this way of thinking that cause organizations to out-perform their competitors. Figure 3-4 shows what it would look like if executives were instead focused on non-zero-sum, long-term management thinking and practice. Data points near the center indicate a perception of consistency with the Caux Round Table *Principles for Business.* Instead of marginalizing stakeholders interests and driving them apart, people work more closely together to better satisfy customers. This, in turn, leads to increased prosperity for all key stakeholders and also increases the value of the enterprise.

## Figure 3-4

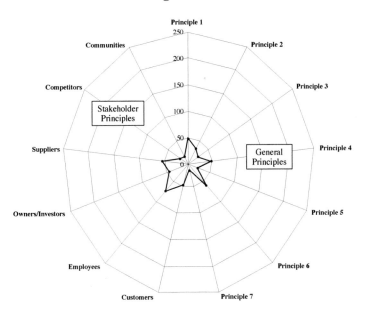

Figure 3-4 reflects a lower cost, more efficient, and better balanced business. In comparison, zero-sum, short-term, shortcut-driven management thinking and practice is a much higher cost, unbalanced way to do business. That is why "Toyoda Precepts," "Guiding Principles at Toyota," and "Contribution Towards Sustainable Development" are so important to Toyota executives. That is why it is so important for executives to adopt and live by explicitly stated non-zero-sum multilateral principles such as the Caux Round Table *Principles for Business.*

Let's again turn to music. What would the Lean view of problems and non-zero-sum, long-term, principle-driven management thinking and practices sound like if we could hear it? It would, of course, be a great piece of music played using many instruments, because the stakeholders are working together – teamwork – instead of against each other. It would sound like Bach's Brandenburg Concerto No. 3. Much greater skills are needed by musicians to play this piece of music. Likewise, there is real skill in possessing the Lean view of problems and non-zero-sum, long-term, principle-driven management thinking and practices.

Executive decision point #5 for sustaining Lean management:

> Lean management requires leaders to recognize and understand problems. Ignoring problems is a shortcut. Can you commit to a Lean view of problems? Yes or no?

Executive decision point #6 for sustaining
Lean management:

> Lean management requires leaders to recognize
> and respond to the key stakeholders. Recognizing
> only investors is a shortcut. Can you commit to
> recognizing stakeholders? Yes or no?

 Executive decision point #7 for sustaining
Lean management:

> Lean management requires leaders to adhere
> to business principles. Having no explicit
> business principles is a shortcut. Can you
> commit to using multilateral, non-zero-sum
> business principles? Yes or no?

# 4 Diving to the Bottom

A lot of questions have been answered so far, but we still have some distance to go to better understand why it is so difficult for executives to sustain Lean management. There is abundant evidence now that proves the Lean management system works and yields much better financial and non-financial results than conventional management. But despite efforts to make this information known to executives, they still resist. Why is that? It seems that executive resistance runs to much deeper intellectual and emotional levels than we have previously considered.

Three things are obvious whenever attempts are made to introduce a new management system:

- It is mischaracterized, misunderstood, and seen as a threat to executives' power.
- It introduces new and unfamiliar concepts, and is perceived as more work.
- It challenges executives' basic beliefs, which they don't want to bother with.

What are the Lean concepts that seem to cause troubles? They include the following nine items:

- Continuous Improvement
- Respect for People
- Stakeholders
- Waste, Unevenness, Unreasonableness
- Non-Zero-Sum

- Sharing
- Takt Time
- Level Loading
- People are Not the Problem

Let's take these one at a time. We know from looking at current state value stream maps that executives don't really believe in continuous improvement, despite what they may say. They see it as ineffective gradualism and prefer "home runs," "game changers," and the "one best way." Wasteful current state value stream maps also clearly indicate that people are not respected, particularly employees, suppliers, customers, and investors.

Executives tend to be strongly focused on satisfying shareholders' interests, and are much less interested in satisfying the interests of the other four key stakeholders. They are unaware of waste, unevenness, unreasonableness – again, just look at a current state value stream map. They are committed to zero-sum thinking and management practices, which means they are not good at sharing. Takt time and level loading mean nothing in a batch-and-queue processing and fundamentally work against sellers' market push production systems.

Just about every executive knows that people *are* the problem, not the bad processes which they are part of. Not living by the "Respect for People" principle is a shortcut that enables executives to consistently cite people as the problem. These nine items are indeed quite troublesome!

Executive decision point #8 for sustaining
Lean management:

> Lean management requires leaders to believe in
> and practice Lean concepts. Not doing so is a
> shortcut. Can you commit to Lean concepts?
> Yes or no?

If Lean management is perceived as a threat, more work, and impinges upon one's belief system, then executives will run from Lean as fast as they can. If they are unable to do that they will find ways to oppose it for as long as they can [1]. If they can't oppose Lean, then they will cherry-pick the Lean principles and practices that they think best apply to their situation and which will be the least disruptive.

The first thing to go is the "Respect for People" principle, called "Cooperation" in the days of Scientific Management [2, 3]. That is tossed out in an instant because zero-sum, shortcut trained executives have no idea how to deal with that. It is too hard for them to understand because it removes them from the realm of black-or-white and interferes with sense-making. From there, executives, being a conservative bunch, will play it safe and cherry-pick various processes and tools that deliver the greatest gains quickly. Along the way, they will most certainly misuse these processes and tools. And they will distort or mangle the meaning of Lean management, fuse it with Six Sigma, etc.

They will also cherry-pick where they apply the cherry-picked Lean processes and tools. Since Lean management has it roots in operations, they will start in operations. The president will proclaim how important this new Lean "initiative" is to the company, and then proceed to let 70 percent of the people in the company off the hook. The people in finance, human resources, corporate communications, legal department, new product development, purchasing, etc., won't have to use the cherry-picked Lean processes and tools. Sometime later they will realize the mistake, but it is usually too late at that point. Too much time has passed and perceptions of Lean as a "manufacturing thing" have solidified.

What has been created is a low-resolution image of Lean management, one that will surely deliver some sort-term gains, but which will inevitably lead to the face a crisis, fix it, face another crisis, fix it, face another crisis, fix it problem. So what does REAL LEAN look like compared to FAKE Lean if we were to see it in the form of a photograph? Figure 4-1a shows a photo of a cute little kitten. Figure 4-1b shows the same photo with lower resolution and high contrast. The cute little kitten in this picture is hardly recognizable. That is what happens when executives cherry-pick Lean. They create a version of Lean that bears little or no resemblance to REAL LEAN. This is a big mistake.

**Figure 4-1a**          **Figure 4-1b**

If you were to think of cherry-picking Lean processes and tools in musical terms, then imagine hearing a song on an AM radio station in the middle of a Florida summer thunderstorm. You would not get much useful information from what you heard because the music was distorted and disrupted by the thunderstorm. Only pieces of the song would make sense to you, and it would not be enjoyable to listen to, so you would turn off the radio. That is also what people do when Lean does not make sense to them; they tune it out or just turn it off.

 Executive decision point #9 for sustaining Lean management:

> Lean management can't be cherry-picked.
> That's a shortcut. Can you commit to not
> cherry-picking Lean? Yes or no?

Returning to the notion that Lean management is perceived as a threat, perhaps we have long underestimated the level of threat that Lean represents to executives. Maybe it is much greater and also rubs on exposed nerves. Let's take a more critical look to see what Lean is really asking executives to do.

Lean management steals prized possessions and status symbols from executives:

- Knowledge
- Rank
- Selfishness
- Individualism
- Loafing

- Complacency
- Blindness
- Arbitrary Decisions
- Organizational Politics

Lean management steals knowledge from executives. It shows them that they are not as smart as they think and that they have much to learn. Rank is compromised because now executives must be part of kaizen and other process and product improvement teams, working as team members, not company leaders or even team leaders, in order to learn Lean principles and practices. Lean is non-zero-sum, which means executives have to share with their stakeholders, not equally, but in ways that are seen as fair. They are not used to doing that.

Individualism shrinks a bit, just enough to make it uncomfortable, and teamwork increases. Executives, just like any other worker, loaf around and are complacent at times, and also often blind to what is really going on (again, just look at a current state value stream map for proof). Lean executives can't make arbitrary decisions; they must make logical, carefully thought-out decisions consistent with both principles: "Continuous Improvement" and "Respect for People." Finally, Lean steals politics and obsequious behaviors from executives because these are waste [4].

Lean management makes executives see ugly truths. It makes them see that they have not been managing well at all. That's a huge come-down. Lean asks executives to separate themselves from their conventional management peer group; to be different, to think and act differently, to do things differently. They don't want to do that.

Lean asks executives to switch from defense to offense (think football). Conventional management is defensive management (think General Motors), while Lean management is offensive (think Toyota). Executives do not want to take on new and unfamiliar positions. They want to keep playing the side of the line that they have played for the last 15 or 25 years. Lean management also asks executives to be less drivers of workers and much more servant leaders and teachers.

But here is the big one: Lean management is inconsistent with most executives' beliefs about:

- The Corporation – ownership, decision-making authority, purpose, rewards
- Microeconomics – economic man, supply-side
- Politics – democracy, responsibility, self-sufficiency
- Social – status, justice, fairness

These are intellectual and emotional hot-buttons that cause a lot of problems in organizations as well as in society. With regards to corporate ownership, most executives will not acknowledge stakeholders' claims to a business. Shareholders own the business, and that's all there is to it. In Lean management, shareholders are very important, but they are one of five key stakeholders – the other four being employees, suppliers, customers, and communities. The issue is not ownership, but that it takes the participation of all five stakeholders to successfully run a business. Don't forget what happens when you marginalize the interests of any of these stakeholders: they look to get even with you, and that increases costs.

Let's face it; it's a lot easier for an executive to be an autocrat or something close to that (Figure 4-2). Just give orders and hold people accountable for results. But that has severe limitations, not the least of which is never-ending bad business processes. Lean management is much closer to a corporate democracy. That hurts an auotcrat's head; they just don't want to go there. They perceive it as a slower and less effective way to lead and do business. The reality, however, is that a corporate autocracy results in low trust and low satisfaction among stakeholders, while a corporate democracy is fairer and yields higher trust and satisfaction among stakeholders.

**Figure 4-2**

| <u>**Corporate Autocracy**</u> | <u>**Corporate Democracy**</u> |
|---|---|
| • Absolute Power | • Distributed Power |
| • Control Based | • Consensus Based |
| • Strong-Man Rule | • Ruled by the People |
| • Censorship | • Freedom of Expression |
| • Arbitrary Decision Making | • Principle-Driven Decision Making |
| • Preserve Self-Interest | • Preserve the Enterprise |
| • Favor One Stakeholder | • Balance Stakeholder Interests |

Where we're headed now gets even more challenging. Everyone uses value stream maps to map process, identify waste, and target areas for kaizen. This singular use does not do justice to the many other types of information we can extract from value stream maps [5]. In this case, information about markets and the corporate microeconomic policies established by executives.

Figure 4-3 is a current state value stream map showing a

batch-and-queue push production system [6, 7]. Assuming the company depicted in the value stream map is not a monopoly, then it must compete against other companies. That means it is, in reality, serving buyers' markets. Yet the executives are managing the business as if they are serving a sellers' market, as the value stream map clearly shows. In other words, the company's senior managers are producing (actually, overproducing), principally to selfishly satisfy their own interests: to meet internal budget targets and to receive rewards for doing so – and less to satisfy customer demand.

# Figure 4-3

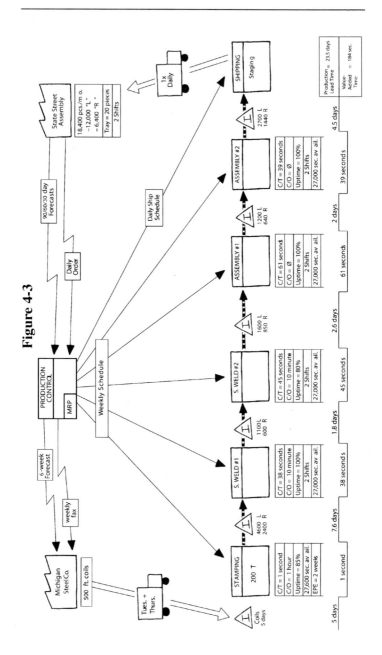

It should be obvious that, given all the waste, unevenness, and unreasonableness shown in Figure 4-3, it is fiscally irresponsible for executives to run a business that way – irrespective of whether this value stream map depicts a manufacturing or service business activities. What is much less obvious is that the current state value stream map, showing inefficient batch-and-queue (push) processing, is a picture of classical and neoclassical microeconomic policy in action.

In other words, the corporate microeconomic policy of the company depicted in Figure 4-3 is supply-side (i.e. supply creates demand) [8]. This microeconomic policy seeks to overproduce and is therefore indifferent to the waste of overproduction – as well as the seven other wastes, plus unevenness and unreasonableness – and therefore is expensive to operate. It is executives, of course, who establish the company's microeconomic policy, whether intentionally or through ignorance. This supply-side policy makes no sense for companies that serve buyers' markets.

Supply-side batch-and-queue processing is out of tune with the marketplace, but very much in tune with so-called rational self-interested maximizers (the company's executives). This exposes the fundamental flaw in supply-side microeconomics: the waste of overproduction, and concomitant higher costs and inefficiencies.

It also exposes a flaw in the concept of "economic man," which most executives subscribe to, because having a free pass to be selfish at both individual and corporate levels damages the business due to higher costs (executive pay and inventories) and slower response to changes in the marketplace. Both are consequences of actions taken by rational self-interested maximizers. Economic man can only make sense if its consequences are free – but they are not free.

We have to ask the uncomfortable question: Is supply-side microeconomics really the key to microeconomic prosperity as classical and neo-classical economists have said [9]? According to standard cost, sellers' market absorption accounting, the answer is "Yes!" However, we all know how terribly flawed standard cost absorption accounting is [10]. It tells us that volume lowers costs, which can lead to lower unit prices and improved price competitiveness, but this encourages wasteful overproduction and increases total costs throughout the supply chain.

This is what happens when generation after generation of executives think they know it all, let other people think for them, and don't question the way they think about and conduct business. As a result, lots of errors are made in trying to contend with a management system that is expensive to operate and responds sluggishly to changes in market conditions.

They may protest and say: "There is no reason to do anything different because our current (conventional or FAKE Lean) management system yields very good financial results." That is certainly true compared to other companies who are managing the same way as they are. But they do not know how much better the company's financial and non-financial performance could be because they lack higher-performing benchmarks for comparison – and which may not yet even exist. With steady application of REAL LEAN management, executives will achieve huge improvements in overall corporate performance.

Figure 4-4 is a future state value stream map showing a pull production system [6]. Assuming the company depicted in the value stream map is not a monopoly, then it must compete against other companies. That means executives recognize the reality that they are serving buyers' markets, and they are managing the business consistent with that market. Great job!

## Figure 4-4

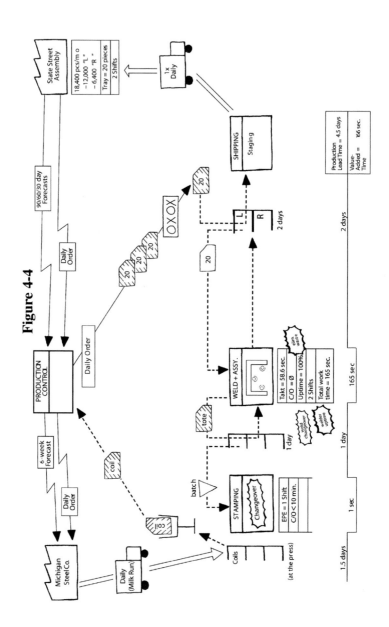

We have a more efficient pull system; a picture of demand-side microeconomic activity. Without all the waste, unevenness, and unreasonableness shown in Figure 4-3, we can see the executives are running the business in a fiscally responsible way – irrespective of whether this value stream map depicts a manufacturing or service business activities. Of course there is still waste, unevenness, and unreasonableness to eliminate, but they have done a good job so far.

Thus, the corporate microeconomic policy of the company depicted in Figure 4-4 is demand-side (i.e. demand creates supply). This microeconomic policy seeks to eliminate the waste of overproduction, as well as the seven other wastes, plus unevenness and unreasonableness, and therefore costs much less to operate. The executives have established a demand-side microeconomic policy that makes sense for competitive buyers' markets. They are in tune with the marketplace. Cost accounting for buyers' market, demand-side microeconomics, also known as Lean accounting, offers an undistorted view of costs and thus greater chances for sustained prosperity [11].

The reason why classical and neo-classical supply-side economists have been so successful at pushing aside demand-side microeconomics is because it was not until the mid-1970s that a complete, fully functional, low cost, efficient demand-side management system was created: Toyota's management system. While the Scientific Management system was a breakthrough, it was basically a much more efficient push production system that could respond more quickly to changes in market demand, but it remained substantially supply-side in its orientation. Henry Ford's flow production system, while a huge improvement in production process methodology, also remained substantially supply-side (sellers' market) in its orientation because of its inability to handle variety. It was not a market-driven pull production system.

Unfortunately, conservative economists and socio-political ideologues don't study the fine details, nuances, and interconnections of management and production systems. Therefore, they incorrectly assume there is no difference between conventional management practice and the Lean management system – REAL LEAN management. Lean is new, within the past 35 years, and competes against a supply-side, sellers' market management system that has been with us for over 200 years and has undergone mostly minor, gradual improvements. The standard cost absorption accounting system that goes with it has been around for over 100 years. These stand as formidable barriers to rational change.

So do Toyota or any other REAL LEAN company operate their business completely according to demand-side microeconomics? No, because companies do not exist in a perfect world. They do operate their business substantially according to demand-side microeconomics, but not completely. Recall that Toyota has about a 30-day supply of vehicles in the U.S. market [12]. This means that Toyota is approximately 92 percent demand-driven and 8 percent supply-side [13]. In other words, Toyota's microeconomic policy for running its business is a blend of both demand-side and supply-side microeconomics (up to 8 percent overproduction). That is what works in the real world. If inventory turns are more than 12, then greater success has been achieved with the demand-side management system.

The corporate microeconomic policy for sustaining the Lean management system is demand-side plus 8 percent or less supply-side. We will denote this unique blend of microeconomic policy using the symbol:

It is pronounced: ek-oh nomics.

But there is a problem. The vast majority of executives characterize themselves as fiscally conservative (though current state value stream maps prove them wrong), and are big believers in supply-side microeconomics. Supply-side microeconomics makes much more sense to executives who have to worry about productive capacity and what to do with it. Supply-side is something they can control and to them appears to be lower risk. It is therefore more acceptable for supply to create demand. They'll reason they have already taken on a lot of risk by having created all that productive capacity, and they don't want to take on any more risk. Demand-side microeconomics appears to them to be more uncertain, and therefore, higher risk.

It is well known that managers and workers involved in a Lean transformation have a tough time adjusting to seeing hours or days worth of work-in-process and finished goods inventories compared to weeks or months worth of inventory laying around. They have a hard time thinking they are not going out of business or will lose orders because of low inventories. They are always more comfortable having more inventory. The standard cost accounting system that just about every company uses fits perfectly with supply-side microeconomics. It rewards managers for overproducing, so why not just do what you are rewarded for doing? Why fight it?

The current state value steam map shown in Figure 4-3 reveals another important thing. It is, on a small (firm-level) scale, a planned economy – a feature normally associated with state-run socialist or communist macroeconomic policy [14]. Who is doing the planning in Figure 4-3? An autocratic central office [15], run by specialists, and aided by a computer system (MRP; material requirements planning). People generally adhere to the production schedule after it has been established, despite changes in market conditions. This clearly reflects the dogged pursuit of a self-interested maximizer, truly at any cost. In addition, they are interfering with the market and distorting the actual customer demand by batching the work and overproducing.

Planned economies are derided by classical and neo-classical economists. It is the complete opposite of their much-loved *laissez faire* brand of capitalism [16]. Lean, on the other hand, is not a planned economy by virtue of the fact that is predominantly a make to the actual market demand democratic management system.

Supply-side corporate microeconomic policy can always be equated with the waste of overproduction. But can demand-side corporate microeconomic policy always be related to underproduction? No; not within the context of Lean management because Lean is not a zero inventory (or negative inventory) management system. Taiichi Ohno said [17]:

"To be sure, if we completely eliminate inventories, we will have shortages of goods and other problems. In fact, reducing inventories to zero is nonsense... In no way is the Toyota production system a zero-inventory system."

 Executive decision point #10 for sustaining Lean management:

> Lean management can't function on the supply-side. That's a shortcut. Can you commit to demand-side microeconomics? Yes or no?

If you are lucky and can get a CEO to accept demand-side microeconomic corporate policy, his or her replacement will most likely favor supply-side microeconomic policy, which will lead to rapid and significant backslide. We can now see how changes in executives derail Lean efforts, not just because they do not know about Lean management, but also because they have fundamentally different views of what the corporation's microeconomic policy should be.

Another challenge is that management reforms are probably viewed by top executives, most of whom say they are conservative, as liberal policy. That's a turnoff. It would be tough to convince them that Lean is actually conservative (fiscally responsible) and that conventional management is liberal (fiscally irresponsible); that Lean offers more economic freedom than conventional management; and, that Lean satisfies self-interests better than conventional management whose direct focus is self-interest.

Instead of recognizing these realities and improving, we spend our time fighting over labels and calling each other names. Free market capitalists disparage progressives, liberals, and socialists, and vice versa, in a never-ending struggle that simply adds cost without creating any value. We cling to our bedrock ideas and make them part of our identity. Either-or choices are presented to us as the right way to think and align ourselves, forcing us to choose sides. We cannot imagine that these either-or choices are false ones, basically linear $y = f(x)$ over-simplifications, and that a pragmatic solution would be to share features of the main ideologies, for each contains some that is good, and avoid that which we know causes harm.

So let's re-frame the problem and make two analogies to better understand how to move forward. Figure 4-5a is an iron-carbon phase diagram while Figure 4-5b shows the mechanical properties of different iron-carbon alloys. You're probably saying: "What the heck are they doing in this book?" It is to emphasize an important point related to sustaining Lean management.

**Figure 4-5b**

**Figure 4-5a**

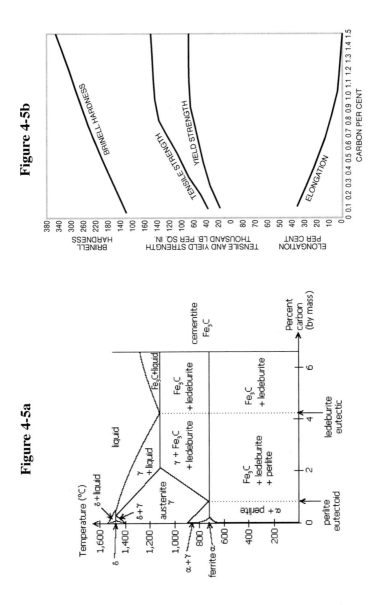

Pure iron is not a very useful material for industrial applications because it has low strength. But adding carbon up to about 2 percent results in an alloy called steel, which is very useful. The really useful steels have carbon contents between 0.1 and 0.8 percent. Figure 4-5b shows the strength and hardness of steel as a function of carbon content. Notice that the strength and hardness greatly increase from 0.1 to 0.8 percent carbon (0.8 percent carbon being the "pearlite eutectoid"). The point is a little alloying with carbon results in something much more useful than pure iron or iron that contains greater than 2 percent carbon. So there is a specific range of carbon content that yields the most useful materials. More or less carbon results in alloys that are less useful.

What if we were to base our company's microeconomic policy on a pragmatic alloy of demand-side microeconomics and 0.5-8 percent of supply-side (192 to 12 inventory turns)? Based on what we see with our own eyes in the real world, it would seem to work better than if we based our company's microeconomic policy on greater concentrations of supply-side microeconomics. Of course, a lot goes into making a high quality demand-side/supply-side alloy. But if Toyota can do it, so can others. After all, they are just people.

Consistent with this alloying concept as a means to find a more useful balance of properties in our microeconomic business system, what if we add to our capitalist ideas a little bit of sharing of the wealth – not necessarily equally divided, but enough so that the five key stakeholders judge the outcome to be fair. Of course we would have to put a lot of effort into maintaining and improving the outcomes, but that's fine because our company would benefit as well as our key stakeholders.

With our capitalist ideas firmly in mind, what if we add to our alloy some sharing of power, authority, and control, much in the same way that Toyota management shares power, authority, and control with workers. While were at it, it would be wise to also share some power, authority, and control with our suppliers and customers, because they are important stakeholders and they know many things that can help all of us. We would no doubt have something better than if we did not do these things.

Another way to think of this is, if you're making soup, you need some major ingredients such as water, vegetables, and meat. If that's all that was in your soup it would not taste very good, but you would certainly eat it if you were hungry. To make it taste better you would add some salt. How much salt would you add? Try 75 percent? No. Maybe 25 percent? No. How about 3.5 percent? No, because then you would have soup with a concentration of salt that is the same as seawater. You probably would not eat it. You would add 0.5 to 2 percent salt – no more than that. Now, the soup you have made tastes great, and you can make it taste even better by adding small concentrations of spices.

The point of this is that alloying and proper concentrations of additives can be a useful concept for understanding how executives must adjust their beliefs about business in preparation for Lean management when it comes to:

- The Corporation – ownership, decision-making authority, purpose, rewards
- Microeconomics – supply-side, rational self-interested maximizer

- Politics – democracy, responsibility, self-sufficiency
- Social – status, justice, fairness

However, most executives are very firm in their beliefs and have long ago hammered their ideological stakes into the ground. There is not much you can do when executives dogmatically cling to their beliefs and refuse to entertain adjustments to their beliefs or entirely new ones.

Taiichi Ohno cautioned executives against mental rigidity in production (and hence financial) plans and in their day-to-day work activities [18]:

> "Sticking to a plan once it is set up is like putting the human body in a cast. It is not healthy... But as long as we cannot accurately predict the future, our actions should change to suit changing situations."

> "I urge all managers... to be more flexible in their thinking as they go about their work."

It is not impossible to get executives to uptake the required new beliefs [19]. Toyota and other REAL LEAN companies do it everyday when they hire outsiders for management positions. But the new hires must want to learn and practice Toyota's management system, which is the starting point for adjusting old beliefs or gaining the new beliefs. If not, they're out of a job.

Executive decision point #11 for sustaining
Lean management:

Lean management requires leaders to accept
"alloying" of corporate, economic, political,
and social systems. Dogmatically favoring
one over others is a shortcut. Can you commit
the concept of alloying? Yes or no?

# 5 Sharing is Fundamental

Sharing is absolutely fundamental to Lean – not necessarily equally, but in ways that the key stakeholders will recognize as fair. We would prefer to be selfish as individuals and corporations, as the long-wave current state has clearly shown. However, to make progress we sometimes have to do the opposite of what we feel like doing. With that in mind, let's explore sharing further to make sure we understand it fully in the context of Lean management and how it relates to social, political, and microeconomic systems.

Question 1: Is sharing socialism? Is the Golden Rule – "Do unto others as you wish be done to you" – socialism? The answer is: "No." Toyota's non-zero-sum management system shares the wealth and seeks fairness among the key stakeholders to ensure they do not increase costs though opportunistic behaviors or try to get even for perceived injustices. Instead it helps them stay focused on satisfying customers, and includes rules to remove "free riders." This is a pragmatic, conservative approach to business, and is clearly rooted in capitalism because it requires people to contribute before they can receive any benefits.

Question 2: Were the people who created Toyota's Management system socialists? The answer is: "No." But don't take my word for it. Here is what Kiichiro Toyoda, the first President of Toyota Motor Corporation, had to say about business and economics in the fall of 1945, soon after Japan's loss in World War II, and eight years after the company was founded [1]:

"We have finally come to the point where Japan will have to convert to a free market economy like that of the United States and compete with the rest of the world on an equal basis. We must therefore reform our protected and monopolistic companies.

The Japanese auto industry has been fostered and protected in a controlled economy and has never braved the rough waves of a free market situation... Moreover, viewed impartially from a global standpoint, Toyota is far from being a first-class company... we should see ourselves as something like a third-class auto company.

We will find it difficult to hold a clear course without foundering [sic] in the stormy seas of a free market economy. The ability of this company, which has sustained heavy blows, to make the transition from a controlled to a free market economy will determine its ultimate success or failure.

However, if we can succeed in a free market economy, we will have a bright future ahead of us. Everything depends upon our own determination."

This passage is representative of the capitalist mindset that had long been part of the Toyoda family corporate business activities [2]. Toyoda is quick to accept corporate reform and a free market economy in Japan, and the need to compete in the buyers' market of automobile sales.

Taiichi Ohno is credited with creating Toyota's production

system, and also turning Kiichiro Toyoda's idea of Just-in-Time into practical reality. Here is what Mr. Ohno had to say about business and economics [3]:

> "The world has already changed from a time when industry could sell everything it could produce to an affluent society where material needs are routinely met. Social values have changed. We are now unable to sell our products unless we think ourselves into the very hearts of out customers, each of whom has different concepts and tastes...
>
> We discovered that industry has to accept orders from each customer and make products that differ according to individual requirements...
>
> It has become a matter of course for customers, or users, each with a different value system, to stand in the frontline of the marketplace and, so to speak, *pull* the goods they need, in the amount and at the time they need them."

Ohno clearly embraces capitalism, repudiates planned economies, and criticizes companies in competitive industries that think they are in a sellers' market. He is unambiguous in his recognition that auto sales are a buyers' market.

Toyota's production system, indeed its entire management system, is built around serving buyers' markets. Conversely, conventional management, a relic of the 1880s, is built around serving sellers' markets, which is much more expensive to do. Yet it has remained the entrenched management system.

Question 3: Are Toyota executives liberal or conservative?
First, let's examine the dictionary definitions of liberal and
conservative [4]:

> con • ser • va • tive – 1. Favoring traditional views
> and values; tending to oppose change. 2. Traditional
> or restrained in style. 3. Moderate; cautious.

> lib • er • al – 1. a. Not limited to or by traditional,
> orthodox, or authoritarian attitudes or dogmas; free
> from bigotry; b. Favoring proposals for reform, open
> to new ideas for progress, and tolerant of the ideas
> and behaviors of others; broad-minded.

Toyota executives have, for decades, been characterized by
the business press and academics as conservative [5]. In
2003, Fujio Cho, the Chairman of Toyota Motor Corporation
said [6]:

> "The worst evil is not changing –
> there is nothing worse than doing nothing."

This quote represents a view that is widely shared among
Toyota executives. So are Toyota executives liberal or conservative? Well, it seems they are liberal. We also know they
recognize stakeholders; they recognize interdependencies;
they care about sharing and fairness (less so about equality);
they are reform-minded; and they think long-term. But
Toyota is not a welfare machine. We're going to have to dig
a bit deeper to answer this question.

What is Toyota's corporate purpose? Is it to make a lot of

money? No. Is it to maximize shareholder value? No. Is it to make cars? Not quite. So, what is it? Toyota's corporate purpose is to "enrich society through car making" [7]. A more descriptive account is as follows [8]:

- Well-Balanced Corporation: to make decisions in a manner consistent with balancing the key and sometimes conflicting objectives of Toyota to serve the greater good of the global communities
- Employee Care: to meet Toyota's obligation and duties to the employees
- Community Care: to meet Toyota's obligation to the local communities

Why is being a well-balanced corporation important? To be out of balance creates waste, unevenness, and unreasonableness, which make it difficult to do anything. For example, think of Enron. Why are employee and community care important? It is because they are the basis for serving customers; you need employees working at a location in harmony with one another.

To understand if Toyota executives are conservative or liberal, we have to examine the "Toyoda Precepts," "Guiding Principles at Toyota," and "Contribution Towards Sustainable Development," and discern what role they play. Please go to Toyota's corporate Web site so that you can read and study these documents yourself [9].

The role these documents play is to guide business activities and executive decision-making. The "Toyoda Precepts" are comparable to the U.S. Constitution. The "Guiding Principles at

Toyota" are comparable to amendments to the U.S. Constitution. The "Contribution Towards Sustainable Development" is comparable to the Declaration of Independence – but it is actually a declaration of *mutual dependence* among the five key stakeholders: customers, employees, suppliers, shareholders, and global society/local communities.

If you examine these documents closely, as well as other sources of information, you'll find that Toyota executives are neither liberal nor conservative; they seem to be both. They seem to be conserberal:

> con • ser • ber • al – 1. Possessing both conservative and liberal views and values. 2. Traditional and reform-minded, cautious yet aggressive.

But most of all, they are realistic and pragmatic. It is no wonder why Fujio Cho, the Chairman of Toyota Motor Corporations says [10]:

> "Our way of thinking is very difficult to copy or even to understand."

Indeed, it is much easier for any person to be fully one thing or another, and not both simultaneously. This places a demand on executives that most have walked away from, as history has shown.

So what is the point of having a corporate purpose, business principles, etc. Let's first look at Figure 5-1 [11]. It is a self-check device attached to a stamping machine that sorts good parts from defective parts. Parts that are too thick are diverted to the upper tray; parts that are too thin are diverted to the lower tray; and parts that are the correct thickness accumulate in the middle tray.

**Figure 5-1**

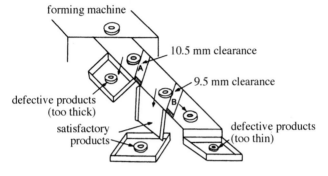

Figure 5-2 illustrates the importance of corporate purpose and non-zero-sum business principles – which are the minimum that any company should have [12]. If used correctly these also function as a self-check device attached to the management system that sort good executive ideas and assumptions from defective executive ideas and assumptions. These help a company and its people stay out of trouble; to avoid unforced errors (compare Figures 3-2 and 3-4). Spending money to fix these errors is waste because it adds cost but creates no value for customers.

Corporate purpose and business principles are not theory. They are pragmatic and helpful guides for business activities and executive decision-making. But few companies have articulated a corporate purpose, and fewer still subscribe to non-zero-sum business principles.

**Figure 5-2**

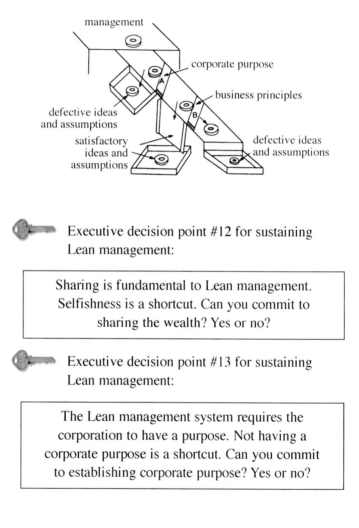

Executive decision point #12 for sustaining
Lean management:

Sharing is fundamental to Lean management.
Selfishness is a shortcut. Can you commit to
sharing the wealth? Yes or no?

Executive decision point #13 for sustaining
Lean management:

The Lean management system requires the
corporation to have a purpose. Not having a
corporate purpose is a shortcut. Can you commit
to establishing corporate purpose? Yes or no?

# 6 We Need Good Students

In order to be good at Lean management, executives have to be good students and faithful practitioners – at the same time. However, history tells us that most executives do not want to become students again. That is *prima facie* evidence of a lack of commitment to continuous improvement, both personally and for their areas of workplace responsibility.

So what does it mean to be a good student? What are the general characteristics of good students? They include:

- Thinks
- Curious
- Studious
- Self-Motivated
- Logical
- Evidence- and Fact-Based
- Disciplined
- Asks Questions
- Interacts with Teachers
- Likes to Learn
- Makes Connections
- Handles Ambiguity
- Desire to Understand
- Respects Teacher and Process
- Humble About Knowledge
- No Cheating
- No Shortcuts
- Apply What They Learned
- Keeps on Learning

Some students can be a headache to teachers. The teacher can see the student is smart, but the student is inattentive, distracted, disruptive, not interested in the knowledge area, and lacking drive. Their work is missing or incomplete, and they do not study or practice what they have learned.

I'm not describing adolescent students in school; I'm describing adult executives. Unfortunately, executives can be a teacher's worst students. They may even be hostile to knowledge and disdain logic, exhibit arrogance about their lack of knowledge [1], and rely on sophistry to win arguments. In general, they are not good at learning or un-learning. If they have learned, they don't like to practice it.

There is a saying in the Training Within Industry (TWI) method for teaching supervisors how to train workers [2]. It is:

"If the worker hasn't learned, the instructor hasn't taught."

This may be true in the case where the worker reports to a supervisor, because there is a power relationship that induces some level of compliance towards practicing the task that the instructor is trying to teach the worker. Workers who do not do the task could lose their jobs or suffer a pay cuts.

In general, learning is a bilateral activity between teacher and student. The responsibility does not rest entirely upon the teacher.

The situation is very different when the teacher is an outside supplier hired to train executives, many of whom think they know it all (see Chapter 1). The teacher can teach, but the student may not learn for a variety of reasons. And they surely will not learn if they don't practice. That's the bane of teaching music as well; most students don't practice consistently and for long enough to learn. And, they are unwilling to make the many small mistakes that are part of learning something new and gaining proficiency.

One of the jobs of executives (and managers and supervisors) in the Lean Management system is to teach their subordinates. Teachers cannot teach if they have not first learned the material themselves [3]. The criticality associated with executives becoming good students and good Lean practitioners cannot be emphasized enough (see Introduction, endnote [9]).

Resistance will be great because future managers are taught in school and on-the-job to tolerate and even to promote waste, unevenness, and unreasonableness. Handy excuses abound. Executives will surely claim they lack time [4] or have other important things to do. They do have the time, and many of the activities that they think are important are not.

Good students will question the practical utility of "economic man," for example. They will realize that ardent supporters of economic man shun multilateral cooperation because it compromises one's ability to act in accordance with narrow self-interests, in zero-sum fashion, and creates ambiguities in roles and responsibilities. They will also realize that economic man conflicts fundamentally with executives' exhortations for teamwork, which requires people from within and outside the company to cooperate.

Good students will not shrink from the challenge of exploring things that interfere with the natural human desire to characterize things as black-or-white to help quickly facilitate sense-making. They will realize that logic and facts do not have to interfere with sense-making, and that mere opinions are insufficient for leading a business and result in an abundance of mischaracterizations and errors throughout the organization.

Senior managers who call for teamwork [5], yet act in ways that undercut teamwork [6], and whose leadership is opinion-based, rather than fact-based, as educators try to teach their students, are destined to under-perform. Leaders who ignore facts to preserve self-interests and protect their knowledge selfishly imperil themselves and others.

If business, made complex by decades of zero-sum practice and shortcuts, were simplified, and waste, unevenness and unreasonableness were removed, then there would be less need for executives to categorize things simplistically, and they would gain a clearer view of the issues and opportunities that they face. They would become more practical and realistic, but first they must learn to think for themselves (see Chapter 4, endnote [15]).

There is no excuse for executives to not be devoted to practicing Lean management and contributing to steadily improving the business. It is irresponsible to do otherwise. If they can't do what is required of them, then they should step away from management and take on a different role such as individual contributor. It could be the best thing that ever happened to them.

Executive decision point #14 for sustaining
Lean management:

Executives must become good Lean students
and faithful Lean practitioners. Can you commit
being a good student? Yes or no?

# 7 Sustaining the Lean Management Movement

The historical record with respect to the successful advancement of new management systems is poor. This book has highlighted and analyzed the deeper reasons why executives do not rush to a new management system despite its obvious financial, non-financial, and human benefits. This should give the leaders of the Lean management movement much to think about in terms of the strategies and tactics they have used to advance Lean management.

Most books and articles on Scientific Management written 75 or 100 years ago sound so fresh, as if they were written today [1]. It appears we are heading on the same path of putting in a tremendous amount of effort with a high probability of having little success. The long-wave current state is very difficult to escape.

Figure 7-1 summarizes some of the similarities and differences in how the Scientific Management community tried to advance their management system compared to how the Lean management community is trying to advance its management system, as well as some outcomes.

## Figure 7-1

| THEN (early 1900s) | NOW (early 2000s) |
|---|---|
| **Methods** | |
| Create Taylor Society to advance Scientific Management. | Create Lean Enterprise Institute to advance Lean management. |
| Characterizations used: movement, disciples, pilgrims, converts, conversion. | Characterizations used: movement, disciples, converts, conversion, transformation. |
| Tried to get Scientific Management into higher education. | Trying to get Lean management into higher education and secondary school education. |
| Sought federal government support for Scientific Management. | Gained state and federal support for Lean management (e.g. NIST/MEPs). |
| Get out the message by publishing books and papers. | Get out the message by publishing books, papers, and workbooks. Electronic distribution of materials via Internet (blogs, podcasts, etc.), CDs, etc. |
| Exchange information via conferences and seminars. | Exchange information via conferences, seminars, and training sessions. |
| Proliferation of consultants. Incompetent consultants characterized as fakirs, quacks, cranks, and charlatans. Fake Scientific Management is much more common. | Proliferation of consultants. Many incompetent consultants. FAKE Lean is much more common. |
| Measure of success: number of companies, industries, or activities pursuing any form of Scientific Management. | Measure of success: number of companies, industries, or activities pursuing any form of Lean management. |
| **Outcomes** | |
| Scientific Management mischaracterized as tools. | Lean management mischaracterized as tools. |
| Benefits of Scientific Management misunderstood. | Benefits of Lean management misunderstood. |
| Scientific Management advocates with high standards mix with Scientific Management advocates with low standards, which causes confusion among executives and regression to the mean. | Lean management advocates with high standards mix with Lean management advocates with low standards, which causes confusion among executives. Regression to the mean likely in progress. |
| Demise in part due to break-up into sects of Scientific Management and severely criticizing each other due to clashing egos [2]. Advocates forced to choose sides, which introduced wide variation in methods and approach to implementation. | Breaking up into Lean sects: Lean manufacturing, Lean service, Lean management, Lean Sigma, etc. Not yet severely criticizing each other. Ego clashes not too bad so far. Advocates may be forced to choose sides. There is wide variation in methods and approach to implementation. |

As discussed in the Preface, the strategies and tactics in use today are largely the same as those used by Scientific Management system advocates in the early 1900s. Yes, there are some important differences, but it is difficult to say if any will initiate a tipping point for Lean management or if they will be inconsequential.

We always have to worry about flavor-of-the-month hungry executives, fixated on the short-term and addicted to short-cuts. Consultants will take advantage of these enduring weaknesses to sell executives the next new thing, and diminishing Lean management will certainly be part of their go-to-market strategy. They know executives can be like amateur golfers, always looking for the next tool, trick, or gimmick to help them shave a few strokes off their game.

The Lean management movement must address the long-wave current state issues identified in this book if it expects to get to a future state where REAL LEAN management is in more widespread use, and that it can survive the two key disruptions that we know for certain will happen: changes in company ownership and changes in management.

Lean management advocates can more clearly articulate the many adjustments that executives must make and provide comfortable pathways to better manage the transition. They probably have to do this quickly because Lean is approximately in the same place that Scientific Management was after 30 years. It was only 15 years later that The Taylor Society closed and the remnants of Scientific Management were subsumed into general management practice [3].

As if the many challenges we face are not enough, we also face an intractable problem: The marketplace will always produce customers who want inferior, low-fidelity versions of Lean management. And the marketplace will always produce consultants who will gladly respond to that customer's pull and seek to satisfy their demand. Nothing can be done about that.

A way forward that may have great impact would be to explain to executives how it is impossible to be ethical operating a zero-sum management system stuffed with shortcuts [4], and that batch-and-queue processing has many unethical features embedded within it (e.g. waste, unevenness, and unreasonableness) that suggest its abandonment would be a wise course of action.

This ethical dimension could be tied to customers' interest in corporations that sincerely embrace environmental sustainability practices, and thus strengthen the case that it would be wise to abandon zero-sum conventional management.

We must put more effort into getting executives to think in terms of *time* (chronomics) and *information* (infonomics) rather than *money* (economics) [5]. We need to get them to think in terms of *process and results* instead of just *results*. We have to teach executives to see that blaming people for problems is waste and that it increases cycle times and cuts off the flow of information [6]. Doing these things, as well as cultivating new leaders, may help keep the Lean management movement alive beyond the next 15 years.

The question of how to sustain the Lean management movement also has no simple answers and can not be answered by one person. You must participate in this process by gathering more information, observing, trying new things, reflecting, and thinking for yourself. Understanding the root causes of problems and identifying practical countermeasures is your job as well as mine.

# 8 Closing Thoughts

The overall tone of this book may seem harsh to many people. However, some readers will effortlessly look past this fault and instantly recognize my true intent: to help executives improve their performance, and that of their organization, through the practice of REAL LEAN management, so they can better satisfy customers. Think of me as a demanding sensei (teacher), perhaps a bit like Mr. Ohno, whose admonishments are purposeful, not arbitrary, and whose interests sincerely lie in helping others succeed and prosper.

However, it will be very difficult to succeed and prosper if executives keep making the same errors. Musicians, for example, at some point get tired of making mistakes and seek fundamental corrections in their understanding of the music and their technique in order to improve their performance. Executives, on the other hand, are very tolerant of mistakes and keep making the same errors. When will they get sick of making the same errors and seek fundamental corrections in their understanding of business and their management system in order to improve their performance? Hopefully this book will help motivate executives to do exactly that.

One of the principal ideas that readers should take from this book is:

> **Executives must challenge their canonical assumptions about business if they want to make the transition from conventional management to REAL LEAN management.**

These canonical assumptions include:

- Business is zero-sum
- Executives can "know it all"
- Economic man
- Supply-side microeconomics
- Companies exist to maximize shareholder value
- Corporate autocracy is better
- Capitalism can't be alloyed
- Conflict has no costs
- Fairness is not relevant
- Executives don't teach
- Stakeholders don't matter, only investors matter
- Sharing is impractical
- It's OK to operate without corporate purpose and business principles
- Shortcuts are acceptable
- "Respect for People" is optional

None of these items are found in corporate Lean audits and assessments.

In my view, the hot-button social, microeconomic, and political issues discussed in Chapters 4 and 5 do not trample on conservative values of economic freedom and the primacy of individual rights over collective needs. Lean management, understood and applied correctly, results in greater economic freedom and strengthens individuality in ways that cannot be done otherwise [1-3]. These ideologies can coexist in harmony and prosper with mutual respect for one another.

However, when viewed from the customer's perspective, the

executive, who only knows conventional zero-sum management practice [4], the Lean management system looks like a dud; it has a lot of strikes against it. The Introduction identified seven strikes, and dozens more were identified in subsequent chapters. Do top executives really care about Toyota's success, the mindset of its executives, and their methods? I don't think so. They will cite themselves or their company's success as evidence that their management system works quite well, thank you very much. All their company needs is some tweaking to cut costs and improve profitability.

We have to find ways to turn those strikes against Lean into base hits and an occasional home run.

The adjustments that executives must make are many and varied, large and small, easy to get at and buried deep in their hearts and minds. It seems we have greatly underestimated our task. Hopefully this book has clarified the problem of how to sustain Lean management.

The odds seem to favor the Lean management system going the way of Scientific Management, whether it exists within an organization or as a larger movement [5, 6]. That should alarm us and motivate us all to better understand root causes and identify countermeasures, and to share our findings. Formal root cause analyses will surely point us, in part, in the direction of those who educate future executives: school teachers (all levels), current executives, and consultants.

The most amazing thing about Toyota Motor Corporation is its executives' constancy of purpose and commitment to its principled non-zero-sum management system over six generations or so of managers. Toyota executives have long been committed to thinking, flexible in their thinking, not bound by dogmatic ideologies, and are realistic and practical. This has led to long-term prosperity for the company and its key stakeholders.

How can we help make that happen elsewhere? We have to find executives who are willing to commit to the 14 executive decision points for sustaining Lean management. These are summarized as follows:

 1. Lean management requires leaders to serve others, not themselves. Self-serving leadership is a shortcut. Can you commit to servant leadership? Yes or no?

 2. Lean management requires leaders who can admit they don't know it all. Thinking you know it all is a shortcut. Can you admit you don't know it all to yourself and others? Yes or no?

 3. Lean management requires leaders who are willing to learn how to operate a non-zero-sum management system. Can you commit to learning about Lean non-zero-sum management? Yes or no?

 4. Lean management requires executives who will do the work. Can you commit to eliminating the shortcuts? Yes or no?

 5. Lean management requires leaders recognize and understand problems. Ignoring problems is a

shortcut. Can you commit to a Lean view of problems? Yes or no?

 6. Lean management requires leaders to recognize and respond to the key stakeholders. Recognizing only investors is a shortcut. Can you commit to recognizing stakeholders? Yes or no?

 7. Lean management requires leaders to adhere to business principles. Having no explicit business principles is a shortcut. Can you commit to using multilateral, non-zero-sum business principles? Yes or no?

 8. Lean management requires leaders to believe in and practice Lean concepts. Not doing so is a shortcut. Can you commit to Lean concepts? Yes or no?

 9. Lean management can't be cherry-picked. That's a shortcut. Can you commit to not cherry-picking Lean? Yes or no?

 10. Lean management can't function on the supply-side. That's a shortcut. Can you commit to demand-side microeconomics? Yes or no?

 11. Lean management requires leaders to accept "alloying" of corporate, economic, political, and social systems. Dogmatically favoring one over others is a shortcut. Can you commit the concept of alloying? Yes or no?

12. Sharing is fundamental to Lean management. Selfishness is a shortcut. Can you commit to sharing the wealth? Yes or no?

 13. The Lean management system requires the corporation to have a purpose. Not having a corporate purpose is a shortcut. Can you commit to establishing corporate purpose? Yes or no?

14. Executives must become good Lean students and faithful Lean practitioners. Can you commit being a good student? Yes or no?

Making these commitments will help executives build intra- and inter-organizational support for necessary changes in business thinking and practices.


I, _____,
hereby commit to these 14 decision points.



_____     _____

Signature                                    Date

# Endnotes

### Preface

[1] The books are: B. Emiliani, with D. Stec, L. Grasso, and J. Stodder, *Better Thinking, Better Results: Case Study and Analysis of an Enterprise-Wide Lean Transformation*, second edition, The CLBM, LLC, Wethersfield, Conn., 2007; B. Emiliani, *REAL LEAN: Understanding the Lean Management System*, Volume One, The CLBM, LLC, Wethersfield, Conn., 2007; B. Emiliani, *REAL LEAN: Critical Issues and Opportunities in Lean Management*, Volume Two, The CLBM, LLC, Wethersfield, Conn., 2007; and B. Emiliani, *Practical Lean Leadership: A Strategic Leadership Guide for Executives*, The CLBM, LLC, Wethersfield, Conn., 2008

[2] B. Emiliani, *REAL LEAN: Critical Issues and Opportunities in Lean Management*, Volume Two, The CLBM, LLC, Wethersfield, Conn., 2007, Chapters 1-6 and 10

[3] F.W. Taylor, *The Principles of Scientific Management*, Harper & Brothers Publishers, New York, NY, 1911

[4] F.W. Taylor, *Scientific Management: Comprising Shop Management, Principles of Scientific Management, Testimony Before the House Committee*, foreword by Harlow S. Person, Harper & Brothers Publishers, New York, NY, 1947, p. xii

[5] H. Ford with S. Crowther, *Today and Tomorrow*, Doubleday, Page & Company, New York, NY., 1926; T. Ohno, *Toyota Production System: Beyond Large-Scale Production*, Productivity Press, Portland, OR, 1988, and W. Tsutsui, *Manufacturing Ideology: Scientific Management in Twentieth-Century Japan*, Princeton University press, Princeton New Jersey, 1998

[6] J.P. Womack, "Ten Years and Counting," e-mail to the Lean community, 23 October 2007, and J.P. Womack, "Respect for People," e-mail to the Lean community, 20 December 2007, www.lean.org

[7] One thing that is different from the past is the proliferation of books on a wide range of aspects of Lean management (including this one). Knowing the details could make Lean management a lot less attractive. The books could have the effect of raising awareness of just how far a company and its managers have to go, which could be discouraging. The books could intimidate executives because it appears to them as an overwhelming challenge that is not realistic and therefore not worth pursuing. So, despite authors' good intentions, the Lean journey may not look like an attractive opportunity to presidents or CEOs steeped in conventional management

practice. The many books on Lean can create an impression of complexity and lead to confusion. Anything that proceeds in the direction of making things more complex or confusing for executives, whether in fact or in appearance, will likely not be accepted.

[8] These books include: T. Ohno, *Toyota Production System*, Productivity Press, Portland, OR, 1988; Y. Monden, *Toyota Management System: Linking the Seven Key Functional Areas*, Productivity Press, Portland, OR, 1993; M. Cowley and E. Domb, *Beyond Strategic Planning: Effective Corporate Action with Hoshin Planning*, Butterworth-Heinemann, New York, NY, 1997; Y. Monden, *Toyota Production System: An Integrated Approach to Just-In-Time*, third edition, Industrial Engineering and Management Press, Norcross, GA, 1998; S. Basu, *Corporate Purpose: Why it Matters More than Strategy*, Garland Publishing, New York, NY, 1999; B. Maskell and B. Baggaley, *Practical Lean Accounting*, Productivity Press, New York, NY, 2003; T. Fujimoto, *The Evolution of a Manufacturing System at Toyota*, Oxford University Press, New York, NY, 1999; J. Liker, *The Toyota Way*, McGraw-Hill, New York, NY, 2004; S. Hino, *Inside the Mind of Toyota*, Productivity Press, New York, NY, 2006; and B. Emiliani, with D. Stec, L. Grasso, and J. Stodder, *Better Thinking, Better Results: Case Study and Analysis of an Enterprise-Wide Lean Transformation*, second edition, The CLBM, LLC, Wethersfield, Conn., 2007

[9] See for example: J. Liker, *The Toyota Way*, McGraw-Hill, New York, NY, 2004; D. Mann, *Creating a Lean Culture: Tools to Sustain Lean Conversions*, Productivity Press, New York, NY, 2005; J. Liker and D. Meier, *Toyota Talent: Developing Your People the Toyota Way*, McGraw-Hill, New York, NY, 2007; B. Emiliani, with D. Stec, L. Grasso, and J. Stodder, *Better Thinking, Better Results: Case Study and Analysis of an Enterprise-Wide Lean Transformation*, second edition, The CLBM, LLC, Wethersfield, Conn., 2007; J. Liker and M. Hoseus, *Toyota Culture*, McGraw-Hill, New York, NY, 2008; and B. Emiliani, *Practical Lean Leadership: A Strategic Leadership Guide for Executives*, The CLBM, LLC, Wethersfield, Conn., 2008

## Prologue

[1] *The American Heritage College Dictionary*, 3rd edition, Houghton Mifflin Co., New York, 1997, p. 1261

[2] *The American Heritage College Dictionary*, 3rd edition, Houghton Mifflin Co., 1997, p. 190

[3] Some people have difficulty understanding why "zero-sum" is considered a negative in business. Whether or not zero-sum is a negative depends

upon the design of the activity in question. For example, football games are zero-sum (one winner and one loser) by design, and we accept that. It is a rule that defines the system to help achieve desired outcomes. Business is not zero-sum by design. Nowhere is business formally defined as zero-sum. Business school professors, for example, do not explicitly teach business as zero-sum (though in some courses it is implied). Business leaders purposefully make business zero-sum to simplify comprehension and day-to-day (and sometimes strategic) management of a business. The effect of operating a business zero-sum is to create a winner (the company; principally senior management and the shareholders) and many losers (suppliers, employees, customers, and communities). This has the effect of activating stakeholders to work against the company's interests: by slowing down the work, charging higher prices, quality problems, longer lead-times, etc. This, in-turn negatively impacts shareholders, the very people who management was trying to benefit through their use of zero-sum business policies and practices. This is why business is not formally defined as zero-sum; you end up hurting yourself and others. Because it is often difficult to see, and it usually occurs over a period of one, two, or three decades or more, it appears that zero-sum business policies and practices do no harm - but they do indeed do harm. Just look at General Motors' decades-long slide compared to Toyota's decades-long ascension. The former has been dedicated to zero-sum business policies and practices since the 1950s, while the latter has been dedicated to non-zero-sum business policies and practices since its inception in 1937. A company responds better and faster to changes in the marketplace using non-zero-sum business policies and practices. It helps build long-term competitive advantage because people work with you instead of against you. Unfortunately, most executives would rather fight with their stakeholders than work together to satisfy common interests.

[4] "The Toyota Way 2001," Toyota Motor Corporation, internal document, Toyota City, Japan, April 2001

[5] The reality we face is that it could take three slow, time-consuming steps to get executives to understand what "Respect for People" really means. Step 1: Where "Respect for People" means *employees* (see Appendix I and note 8). Step 2: Where "Respect for People" means *stakeholders*. Step 3: Where "Respect for People" means *humanity* (as originally intended). For more on understanding the "Respect for People" principle and its literal translation from Japanese, see the blog posting "Exploring the 'Respect for People' Principle of the Toyota Way" by Jon Miller dated 4 February 2008, http://www.gembapantarei.com/2008/02/exploring_the_

respect_for_people_principle_of_the.html.

[6] B. Emiliani, *Practical Lean Leadership: A Strategic Leadership Guide for Executives*, The CLBM, LLC, Wethersfield, Conn., 2008

[7] *Lean Lexicon*, 3rd edition, version 3.0, Lean Enterprise Institute, Cambridge, MA, September 2006, p. 100

[8] *Ibid*, p. 96

[9] T. Ohno, *Toyota Production System*, Productivity Press, Portland, OR, 1988, pp. 19-20

[10] M.L. Emiliani, "Lean Behaviors," *Management Decision*, Vol. 36, No. 9, pp. 615-631, 1998

[11] M. Rother and J. Shook, *Learning to See*, Lean Enterprise Institute, Boston, MA, 1999

[12] Mr. Ohno said: "I have no intention of criticizing Henry Ford (1863-1947). Rather, I am critical of Ford's successors who have suffered from excessive dependence on the authority of the Ford system precisely because it has been so powerful and created such wonders in productivity. However, times change." See T. Ohno, *Toyota Production System*, Productivity Press, Portland, OR, 1988, p. xiv. While it is important to refrain from blaming people because it conflicts with the "Respect for People" principle, it is reasonable to criticize those who hold or have held top executive positions for their fundamental failures of leadership such as: a) failure to think and to question the efficacy of their management system, or b) failure recognize that times have changed (e.g. from sellers' markets to buyers' markets).

**Introduction**

[1] "The Toyota Way 2001," Toyota Motor Corporation, internal document, Toyota City, Japan, April 2001

[2] B. Emiliani, *REAL LEAN: Understanding the Lean Management System*, Volume One, The CLBM, LLC, Wethersfield, Conn., 2007

[3] FAKE Lean is characterized by a "copypaste" mentality, where executives pick up Lean terms and begin using them without knowing what they mean. The word "copypaste" was provided by Angie Palmer and Luis Fernandez, on 13 October 2007 at Goal International Restaurant in Hartford, Conn.

[4] D. Mann, *Creating a Lean Culture: Tools to Sustain Lean Conversions*, Productivity Press, New York, NY, 2005; B. Emiliani, *REAL LEAN: Understanding the Lean Management System*, Volume One, The CLBM, LLC, Wethersfield, Conn., 2007, Chapter 5; and J. Liker and M. Hoseus,

*Toyota Culture*, McGraw-Hill, New York, NY, 2008

[5] J.P. Womack, "The Problem of Sustainability," e-mail to the Lean community, 30 May 2007

[6] B. Emiliani, with D. Stec, L. Grasso, and J. Stodder, *Better Thinking, Better Results: Case Study and Analysis of an Enterprise-Wide Lean Transformation*, second edition, The CLBM, LLC, Wethersfield, Conn., 2007, pp. 283-290

[7] J. Liker, *The Toyota Way*, McGraw-Hill, New York, NY, 2004 and J. Liker and M. Hoseus, *Toyota Culture*, McGraw-Hill, New York, NY, 2008

[8] N. Shirouzu, "Paranoid Tendency: As Rivals catch Up, Toyota CEO Spurs Big Efficiency Drive," *The Wall Street Journal*, 9 December 2006; C. Fishman, "No Satisfaction at Toyota,"*Fast Company*, Issue 111, December 2006, http://www.fastcompany.com/magazine/111/open_no-satisfaction; and D. Welch, "Staying Paranoid at Toyota," *BusinessWeek*, 2 July 2007, pp. 80-82

[9] The following quote by Teruyuki Minoura, former president and CEO of Toyota Motor Manufacturing North America, explains why it is incorrect to use the DNA analogy: "You might call these tenets [of Toyota and of the Toyota Production System] the 'DNA' of Toyota. I wish they were truly like DNA. Why? Because DNA is genetically encoded and is transmitted automatically from parents to children. If Toyota's core values were truly like DNA, our philosophy and production system would be automatically inherited by future generations of Toyota team members. Unfortunately, it's not that easy. Our philosophy is not really in our genes. The transmission of a fundamental philosophy to new people or to the next generation is normally accomplished through education and training. In Toyota, we call this process 'ikusei.' This concept is closer to 'nurturing or raising,' just as parents raise children, than to simple education or training. Parents raise children through instruction, training, and by setting examples day in and day out. That is what we must do at Toyota, to instill our core philosophies as well as the practical know-how of the Toyota Production System. This notion of 'ikusei' or 'nurturing/raising' is another important underpinning of every Toyota operation... new hires learn about Toyota through lectures and on-the-job training. Training and learning are parts of a life-long process that never cease as long as one works for Toyota. At the same time, Toyota managers are expected to train and nurture their subordinates, just as parents raise their children. This is done through constructive criticisms and problem solving approaches. We even evaluate managers for their ability to nurture and develop their subordinates." Address to the World Class Manufacturing Forum, May 2002,

http://www.electronics-scotland.com/industry_comment/comment _item.cfm?itemID=18. You can think of the elusive nature of the sustainability of Lean in another way: Say you exercise every day for 10 years. At what point will your body begin to automatically exercise by itself? The answer is: "Never." You have to keep working at it; there is no end.

[10] B. Emiliani, *REAL LEAN: Critical Issues and Opportunities in Lean Management*, Volume Two, The CLBM, LLC, Wethersfield, Conn., 2007, Chapters 1-6 and 10, and B. Emiliani, with D. Stec, L. Grasso, and J. Stodder, *Better Thinking, Better Results: Case Study and Analysis of an Enterprise-Wide Lean Transformation*, second edition, The CLBM, LLC, Wethersfield, Conn., 2007, pp. 283-290

[11] B. Emiliani, *REAL LEAN: Critical Issues and Opportunities in Lean Management*, Volume Two, The CLBM, LLC, Wethersfield, Conn., 2007, Chapters 1-6 and 10

[12] B. Emiliani, with D. Stec, L. Grasso, and J. Stodder, *Better Thinking, Better Results: Case Study and Analysis of an Enterprise-Wide Lean Transformation*, second edition, The CLBM, LLC, Wethersfield, Conn., 2007, pp. 283-290

[13] J. Cunningham and O. Fiume, *Real Numbers: Management Accounting in a Lean Organization*, Managing Times Press, Durham, NC, 2003; B. Maskell and B. Baggaley, *Practical Lean Accounting*, Productivity Press, New York, NY, 2004; and J. Huntzinger, *Lean Cost Management: Accounting for Lean by Establishing Flow*, J. Ross Publishing, Ft. Lauderdale, FL, 2007

[14] S. Spear, "Learning to Lead at Toyota," *Harvard Business Review*, May 2004, pp. 78-86; M. Fackler, "The 'Toyota Way' is Translated for a New Generation of Foreign Managers," *The New York Times*, 15 February 2007

[15] N. Shirouzu and S. Moffett, "As Toyota Closes in on GM, Quality Concerns Also Grow," *The Wall Street Journal*, 4 August 2004; and N. Shirouzu, "Toyota Review Reveals Need for More Quality Checks," *The Wall Street Journal*, 11 December 2006

[16] B. Emiliani, *REAL LEAN: Critical Issues and Opportunities in Lean Management*, Volume Two, The CLBM, LLC, Wethersfield, Conn., 2007, Chapters 13, "Lean Enterprise Estate Planning."

## Chapter 1

[1] D. Nelson, "Industrial Engineering and the Industrial Enterprise, 1890-1940," in *Coordination and Information*, N. Lamoreaux and D. Raff, Eds., The University of Chicago Press, Chicago, IL, 1996, pp. 38-43

[2] Company presidents do what is sensible to them. Most are satisfied with the current state of management practice and financial return, and strongly dislike taking risks that could upset the current state and which might also diminish financial returns. Fifty dollars reliably in-hand is better then the promise of $100, according to their logic. Few executives comprehend the wide-ranging benefits of a new management system and transition to it before business conditions deteriorate. Lean management makes more sense to executives when they are desperate.

[3] The common process for promoting managers to executive positions focuses on the selection of people who exude great confidence and who see things in unambiguous terms; i.e. black-or-white, typically zero-sum in its form or substance. Being good at firefighting in the workplace and the "take no prisoners" approach to cost-cutting reflects the desirability of these characteristics. The promotion process generally weeds out people who are good candidates to become Lean leaders because they exhibit leadership characteristics that, on the surface, appear to those in power to be less desirable, including: humility, can admit they do not know it all, admits errors, can deal with ambiguity, and are inclined to ask "why?" when they encounter problems.

[3] H. Gantt, "Influence of Executives," in Modern Manufacturing: A Partnership of Idealism and Common Sense, *The Annals of the Academy of Political and Social Science*, Vol. LXXXV, No. 174, September 1919, p. 257

[4] Compare this to the general characteristics of a REAL LEAN leader: A person who reads – committed to lifelong learning; wants to try what he or she read – curious, seeks to validate the reading; persistent – failure means understand the root cause and try again and again; never stops thinking – problems are a value-laden personal challenge; constantly communicating – likes to teach others; totally consistent and disciplined – variation in leadership is waste; concerned about cause-effect relationships – both task and behavioral; humble and participative – not smarter than everyone else and has much to learn.

[5] Many business and management journals and periodicals report good news or present case studies of success stories. There is less in the way of critical analysis of what went wrong, and even less that investigates problems using formal root cause analysis methods.

[6] Reprinted by permission of *Harvard Business Review*. From "Lessons from Toyota's Long Drive," *Harvard Business Review*, by Thomas A. Stewart and Anand P. Raman, July-August 2007, p. 80. Copyright © 2007 by the Harvard Business School Publishing Corporation; all rights reserved.

[7] "The Toyota Way 2001," Toyota Motor Corporation, internal document,

Toyota City, Japan, April 2001

## Chapter 2

[1] S. Basu, *Corporate Purpose: Why it Matters More than Strategy*, Garland Publishing, New York, NY, 1999

[2] The items listed are collected simply by reading *The Wall Street Journal* for over a decade.

[3] Some executives pick up the moniker "cost-cutting expert" from the business press. But let's face the facts. What they are really doing is sitting in an office and putting lines through budget items, writing down smaller numbers, and handing it off to other people to make it happen. There is no expertise in that; there is no use of the scientific method to understand the true source of problems. The real cost-cutting experts are those executives who understand voice of the customer, and waste, unevenness, and unreasonableness (and participate in its elimination).

[4] See J.S. Mill, *Principles of Political Economy*, Longmans, Green and Co., London, 1848 and http://en.wikipedia.org/wiki/Economic_man

[5] R.W. Cooke-Taylor, the author of *Modern Factory System*, published in 1891, had this to say about economic man: "A whole series of writers presently appeared announcing that as those supposed laws [economic man] were irrefutable in arguments so it was useless to struggle against their fulfillment; that as society was thus deeply diseased political economy had no mission but to insist upon the fact. Many of these were men (and women) of great ability and of kindliest dispositions, yet the accepted this 'ghastly framework' as a true presentation of the necessary lineaments of modern society, and proceeded with alacrity, and even with enthusiasm, to give the finishing touches to the picture. A monster was evolved from their imaginations, the *Economic Man*, with attributes such as never man had, and converted into something like a fetish. This figment was passionless, omniscient, omnipresent, solely actuated by self-interest, and with no necessary past or future. He held no relations with, and acknowledged no obligations to his fellow-man but those of the economical kind; he was touched by no ethic, aesthetic, or spiritual motive. To that appalling model, they seemed to argue, it was the duty of all proper-minded persons to conform... Their [Adam Smith *et al.*] attention was concentrated too much on the subject of their study (wealth), and too little on its object (man)." R. Whatley Cooke-Taylor, *Modern Factory System*, Kegan Paul, Trench, Trubner & Co., Ltd., London, 1891, p. 256 and p. 259

[6] See J.K. Ingram, *A History of Political Economy*, Macmillan and Co.,

New York, NY, 1888. Ingram, who held a Doctorate of Laws degree, had this to say about the poor quality of "economic investigation" from the 1600s to the 1800s (pp. 241-242): "The radical vice of this unscientific character of political economy seems to lie in the too individual and subjective aspect under which it has been treated. Wealth having been conceived as what satisfies [human] desires, the definitely determinable qualities possessed by some objects of supplying physical energy, and improving the physiological constitution, are left out of account [i.e. a shortcut]. Everything is gauged by the standard of subjective notions and desires. All desires are viewed as equally legitimate, and all that satisfies our desires as equally wealth. Value, being regarded as the result of a purely mental appreciation, the social value of things in the sense of their objective utility, which is often scientifically measurable, is passed over, and the ratio of exchange is exclusively considered. The truth is, that at the bottom of all economic investigation must lie the idea of the destination of wealth for the maintenance and evolution of a society. And, if we overlook this, our economics will become a play of logic [i.e. abstract thought experiment] or a manual for the market [i.e. a game], rather than a contribution to social science; while wearing an air of completeness, they will be in truth one-sided and superficial... The laws of wealth must be inferred from the facts of wealth, not from the postulate of human selfishness." In other words, fundamental premises in economics such as "economic man," "natural liberty," "indefeasible rights," etc., lack scientific rigor and therefore may rest on faulty assumptions. Ingram stresses that the people who study economics should strive to become more scientific in their efforts, and less anchored in faulty propositions, because economics will have the practical effect of (p. 246) "...modifying our whole environment, affecting our whole culture, and regulating our whole conduct..." as industrialization advances in the west.

[7] See J. Hammond, R. Keeney, and H. Raiffa, "The Hidden Traps in Decision Making," *Harvard Business Review*, September-October 1998, Vol. 76, No. 5, pp. 47-58 and http://en.wikipedia.org/wiki/Confirmation _bias#Tolstoy_syndrome

[8] E. Thornton, "Perform or Perish," *BusinessWeek*, 5 November 2007, pp. 38-45

[9] B. Emiliani, with D. Stec, L. Grasso, and J. Stodder, *Better Thinking, Better Results: Case Study and Analysis of an Enterprise-Wide Lean Transformation*, second edition, The CLBM, LLC, Wethersfield, Conn., 2007, Chapter 10

## Chapter 3

[1] For over 200 years executives have been concerned about whether or not they are getting the highest output for the wages paid to laborers. They are perpetually convinced that labor costs are too high. So, rather than question their leadership or observe, understand, and improve processes, they obsessively search for ways to lower labor costs. It's almost never a labor wage problem – it is a process problem (and a sales growth problem), as any current state value stream map depicting batch-and-queue processing will tell you. But instead, generation after generation of executives fail to recognize this and instead take shortcuts to lower labor costs.

[2] Executives have difficulty making the transition to Lean management and long-term focus because they are mired in a constant firefight over short-term problems, mostly driven by their own short-term thinking and the shortcuts they take. It is not customary for executives to do root cause analysis of management problems and identify practical countermeasures. Doing so would reduce the amount of short-term firefighting and permit executives to have a longer-term focus. The lack of root cause analyses means problems will recur, and thus keep executive's attention focused on the short-term. They've managed to trap themselves, illustrating how important it is for executives to consistently use formal processes to identify and correct problems.

[3] See "Toyoda Precepts" and the "Toyota Guiding Principles at Toyota" at http://www.toyota.co.jp/en/vision/philosophy/index.html and "Contribution Towards Sustainable Development" at http://www.toyota.co.jp/en/vision/sustainability/index.html

[4] Caux Round Table *Principles for Business*, 1994, http://www.cauxround-table.org/principles.html. Looking at these principles from another direction, they are an excellent resource for informing executives of the most likely areas in which they will stumble.

## Chapter 4

[1] B. Emiliani, *REAL LEAN: Understanding the Lean Management System*, Volume One, The CLBM, LLC, Wethersfield, Conn., 2007, Chapter 16. Despite being educated, the arguments executives make against Lean management are invariably rooted in illogical thinking in order to win the argument. Illogical and deceptive arguments, otherwise known as sophistry, can be very difficult to neutralize when the person making such arguments is in a power position.

[2] F.W. Taylor, *The Principles of Scientific Management*, Harper &

Brothers Publishers, New York, NY, 1911

[3] F.W. Taylor, "Shop Management," *Transactions of The American Society of Mechanical Engineers*, Vol. 25, 1903, pp. 1337-1480

[4] Executives say: "Organizational politics are just part of corporate life. That's just the way it is. There's nothing you can do about it." In contrast, I say: "Organizational politics is the nutrient that turns bad ideas into reality, and makes the workplace more confusing and business processes more complex. There surely is something you can do about it." See M.L. Emiliani, "Lean Behaviors," *Management Decision*, Vol. 36, No. 9, pp. 615-631, 1998 and B. Emiliani, *Practical Lean Leadership: A Strategic Leadership Guide for Executives*, The CLBM, LLC, Wethersfield, Conn., 2008.

[5] The use of value stream maps has been extended to the field of accounting to determine the process costs of a value stream (see B. Maskell, "Costing the Value Stream," Lean Enterprise Institute Value Stream Management Summit, Orlando, FL, March 19, 2001). Value stream maps have also been used to determine the amount of carbon dioxide greenhouse gas generated by processing and transportation (see D. Simons and R. Mason, "Lean *and* Green: Doing More with Less," *ECR Journal*, Vol. 3, No. 1, Spring, 2003, pp. 84-91). They have also been used as a new route for identifying leadership problems and improving leadership effectiveness (see M.L. Emiliani and D.J. Stec, "Using Value Stream Maps to Improve Leadership," *Leadership and Organizational Development Journal*, Vol. 25, No. 8, pp. 622-645, 2004).

[6] Copyright Lean Enterprise Institute (www.lean.org). Used with permission.

[7] Figure 4-3 also shows that multiple generations of executives don't know what is going on out on the shop floor. It's harder to know what is going on in offices, so the situation must be much worse there. Leadership is often blind.

[8] The discussion of supply-side microeconomics and demand-side microeconomics contained in this book is based on their core concepts (the "what," not the "how"). For supply-side microeconomics, the core concept is: supply creates demand. For demand-side microeconomics the core concept is: demand creates supply. How this is achieved in business is often through government actions such as taxation, tax cuts, rebates, incentives, government spending, regulation, money supply, etc., to influence the macro economy. These government activities, or other efforts to influence aggregate supply or demand, are not germane to the analysis contained in this book. We will focus only on firm-level microeconomic policy.

[9] The French Economist Jean-Baptiste Say (1767-1832) is known for Say's Law, which states: there can be no demand without supply; meaning

that prosperity increases by increasing supply not demand. Say's law is not a law but a conjecture. Indeed, there can be demand with no supply. The technical term is called "backordered." Sometimes consumer demand can be great, but supply is limited or non-existent because intermediaries such as manufacturers or distributors ignore or delay responding to the customer's demand so they can continue to exploit their large sunk costs in knowledge and assets related to the supply of goods and services already in production. Citizens demand new or revised government policies and legislation, but government representatives will often ignore these calls for years because it impinges upon someone's selfish interests. In the case of United States federal government activities, the inability of elected officials to supply the legislative services demanded by citizens is called "Washington gridlock," which can destroy wealth through delays and inaction. Thus, there can indeed be demand with no supply.

[10] See J. Huntzinger, *Lean Cost Management: Accounting for Lean by Establishing Flow*, J. Ross Publishing, Ft. Lauderdale, FL, 2007. Overproduction is pervasive, as evidenced by overcapacity in many manufacturing and service industries, as well as the many retail stores such as Dollar Tree, Family Dollar, Ocean State Job Lot, and overstock.com that sell close-out and overstock merchandise purchased from manufacturers for pennies on the dollar. These stores survive on manufacturers' supply-side microeconomic policy. Charles Babbage, the author of *On the Economy of Machinery and Manufactures* (1832), viewed overproduction as an inevitable consequence of competition. He saw overproduction as a good thing because gluts stimulated improvements in manufacturing processes and machinery. See Babbage, pp. 156-157 and 173-174. Babbage, like most executives today, remain focused on unit costs rather than total costs. In addition, they have yet to overcome the fallacy that improvement is borne of dire business conditions. Continuous improvement must be understood as a daily activity, in good times or bad.

[11] See B. Maskell and B. Baggaley, *Practical Lean Accounting*, Productivity Press, New York, NY, 2004

[12] Toyota's downward trend in inventory turns since about 1990 (from about 22 to 12) is largely driven by an increase in sales volume in countries whose sales practice (and customer's preference) is to select a car from those parked on dealers' lots. Inventory turns would be greater if the sales practice was greater in its proportion of make-to-order. This clearly illustrates the need for companies that seek to be Lean to reform sales practices and ensure they are consistent with production process capabilities. Too often, material velocity increases in production but sales executives resist

changing sales practices, which results in the continuation of low inventory turns. See R. Schonberger, *Best Practices in Lean Six Sigma Process Improvement*, John Wiley and Sons, Inc., 2008, p. 123.

[13] In comparison, U.S. automakers have typically had a 60- to 90-day supply of vehicles, or 4-6 inventory turns per year for decades. The difference between 12 inventory turns and 4-6 inventory turns is a 2-3-times increase in work-in-process and finished goods inventory. So, while General Motors can be characterized as 75 percent demand-side and 25 percent supply-side (i.e. up to 25 percent overproduction), the operating cost differential between 12 and 4-6 inventory turns is substantial and responsiveness to changes in market conditions is much more sluggish (for this and other reasons). Therefore, anything more than high single digit percentages of supply-side begins to create significant cost problems. It's like having too much salt in the soup; the concentration of supply-side is too great and causes problems.

[14] It is interesting to see how wealthy people, who normally consider themselves conservative capitalists when it comes to business, exhibit socialist tendencies when it comes to the serious business of family wealth management and estate planning. See R. Frank, "New Status Symbol: Family Mission Statements, *The Wall Street Journal*, 12 October 2007 and J. Black, "For Those Born Rich, Lessons in How to Stay that Way," *The New York Times*, 28 October 2007

[15] Connect this thought of a planned economy and centralized planning to the tendency for executives to think they know it all and can control everything (Chapter 1). Executives who think they know it all are essentially engaged in centralized planning (error-free, of course) by not allowing other people in the company, who are decentralized, to think. According to Teruyuki Minoura, former president and CEO of Toyota Motor Manufacturing North America: "He [Mr. Ohno] never gave us answers. Most of the time he wouldn't even tell us if what we did was good or bad. Now I realize what Mr. Ohno was trying to do. He was trying to make us think deeply -- and think for ourselves." Address to the World Class Manufacturing Forum, May 2002, http://www.electronics-scotland.com/industry_comment/comment_item.cfm?itemID=18. According to Fujio Cho, Chairman of Toyota Motor Corporation: "Education and training of your people is therefore vital... and people must be allowed to think." Speech by Mr. Fujio Cho, "Our Endless Challenge Toward Innovation," Nikkei Global Management Forum, Tokyo, Japan, 21 October 2003.

[16] Ever think about what would happen if *laissez faire* were applied to

parenting? The children would be allowed to come home and do illegal drugs until it ruins their life, then seek rehab. This, of course, would prove that the free markets are working properly. That fact that there is no responsibility and accountability apparently is immaterial. It is a fallacious (i.e. no-lose) argument to say that making errors and recovering from errors proves that the market is working, or that bad efficiency that leads to failure is equivalent to good efficiency that leads to recovery. The arguments supporting efficient markets are diminished by the existence of markets for bad ideas, stupidity, fraud, etc. People who criticize free market capitalism face unimaginative, hackneyed, and flawed rejoinders from its supporters, principally: "You're a socialist." This is the equivalent of saying: "Your mother wears army boots." It is an illogical form of argumentation known as an *ad hominem* (against the person) attack, and, more generally, critics must contend with defenders' incessant sophistry. See *Being Logical*, D.Q. McInerny, Random House, New York, NY, 2005

[17] T. Ohno with S. Mito, *Just-In-Time for Today and Tomorrow*, Productivity Press, Cambridge, MA, 1988, p. 24

[18] T. Ohno, *Toyota Production System: Beyond Large-Scale Production*, Productivity Press, Portland, OR, 1988, pp. 46, 52, and 115

[19] There is increasing evidence that conservative or liberal views are hard-wired into the brain (see M. Wenner, "Political Preference is Half Genetic," LiveScience.com, 28 May 2007). However, it appears this hard wiring can be short circuited if people receive continuous training in Lean management and apply what they have learned every day.

**Chapter 5**

[1] Toyota: *A History of the First 50 Years*, Toyota Motor Corporation, Toyota City, Japan, 1988, pp. 95-96

[2] Prior to automobile manufacturing, Toyoda was in the loom manufacturing and spinning and weaving businesses. Since the 1910s, these businesses competed on a global basis in free markets. See *Toyota: A History of the First 50 Years*, Toyota Motor Corporation, Toyota City, Japan, 1988, pp. 23-48 and K. Wada and T. Yui, *Courage and Change: The Life of Kiichiro Toyoda*, Toyota Motor Corporation, Toyota City, Japan, 2002, pp. 109-190

[3] T. Ohno, *Toyota Production System: Beyond Large-Scale Production*, Productivity Press, Portland, OR, 1988, p. xiv

[4] *The American Heritage College Dictionary*, 3rd Edition, Houghton Mifflin Co., New York, 1997, p. 296 and 781

[5] S. Lohr, "Toyota: Innovative and Conservative," *The New York Times*,

15 February 1983; A. Taylor, "How Toyota Copes With Hard Times," *Fortune*, 25 January 1993; J, Gapper, "Toyota Forges Ahead," *Financial Times*, 22 September 2004; J. Liker, *The Toyota Way*, McGraw-Hill, New York, NY, 2004, p. 42; "Fortunes Diverge at Sony, Toyota in Line With Management Styles," *Nikkei*, 18 December 2006; I. Rowley, "Recession Worries Weigh on Toyota," *BusinessWeek*, 5 February 2008

[6] See K. Whitfield, "3 Future Takes from Japan's Big 3," *Automotive Design and Production*, http://www.autofieldguide.com/articles /120303.html

[7] See "Message from Top Management: Harmony with People, Society, and the Environment," http://www.toyota.co.jp/en/vision/message/, January 2008

[8] S. Basu, *Corporate Purpose: Why it Matters More than Strategy*, Garland Publishing, New York, NY, 1999

[9] "Toyoda Precepts" and "Toyota Guiding Principles at Toyota" at http://www.toyota.co.jp/en/vision/philosophy/index.html and "Contribution Towards Sustainable Development" at http://www.toyota.co.jp/en/vision/sustainability/index.html

[10] P. Day, "'Mr. Toyota' is Shy About Being Number One," *BBC News*, 25 June 2007, http://news.bbc.co.uk/2/hi/business/6237110.stm

[11] S. Shingo, *Zero Quality Control: Source Inspection and the Poka-Yoke System*, Copyright 1986 by Taylor & Francis Group LLC - Books. Reproduced with permission of Taylor & Francis Group LLC - Books in the format Tradebook via Copyright Clearance Center.

[12] Executives need to determine their company's corporate purpose. If you come up with a zero-sum based corporate purpose, or something like "our corporate purpose is to make money," you get an "F" and must start over. Hint: study Toyota's corporate purpose.

**Chapter 6**

[1] S. Jacoby, *The Age of American Unreason*, Pantheon Books, New York, NY, 2008

[2] J. Huntzinger, "The Roots of Lean," http://www.superfactory.com/articles/Huntzinger_roots_lean.pdf, June 2005

[3] J. Liker and D. Meier, *Toyota Talent: Developing Your People the Toyota Way*, McGraw-Hill, New York, NY, 2007

[4] Here is a reference point regarding having time to learn Lean: I have been playing the bass guitar for 1.5-3 hours per day, virtually every day, since April 2003. With no prior musical experience to draw upon and no

lessons, I taught myself 90 rock-and-roll songs by summer 2007. While I was doing this I taught 3-4 unique courses per semester; served on two university committees (I actually attended the meetings); was a journal editor for two years and a member of three editorial boards; conducted Lean leadership training workshops for executives and frequently spoke to executive teams; wrote and published five books; wrote 18 peer-reviewed papers; gave 22 presentations and seminars; and was a good husband, father, cook, and gardener. It is a lot easier to learn Lean management than to learn a musical instrument when you work full-time and have all these other activities going on, because you learn Lean mostly on-the-job. So if executives are at work for 10 or 12 hours a day, they can learn and apply Lean principles and practices for 10 or 12 hours a day. The "I don't have time to learn Lean" excuse is indefensible.

[5] Executives are famously disdainful of teamwork amongst themselves (*prima facie* evidence being the highly political nature of most organizations), which is one reason why they do not like to participate on kaizen teams.

[6] Some examples of the ways in which executives undercut teamwork include: favoring one person or function (i.e. finance) over others (such as purchasing); favoring ideas, knowledge, or insights from external sources such as consultants over internal experts; singling out people for blame or praise; segregating people by function (i.e. engineering people located in one building, while sales and marketing people are located far away in another building); establishing a team to investigate a problem and then steering the team towards the outcomes that are acceptable to management; establishing a team to validate management's pre-conceived solutions to a problem; etc.

### Chapter 7

[1] B. Emiliani, *REAL LEAN: Critical Issues and Opportunities in Lean Management*, Volume Two, The CLBM, LLC, Wethersfield, Conn., 2007, Chapters 1-6 and 10

[2] They became "player haters," disrespecting each other and generally exhibiting wasteful behaviors towards their peers.

[3] In an odd twist of fate, the last hurrah of Scientific Management turned out to be the management course that Homer M. Sarasohn and Charles A. Protzman taught to Japanese executives starting in 1949. Their course, "The Fundamentals of Industrial Management: CCS Management Course" was well-received by executives eager to learn about American industrial management. Of the three books drawn upon to create the course, two were deeply rooted in Scientific Management: D. S. Kimball, *Principles of*

*Industrial Organization*. New York: McGraw-Hill, 1939 and L. P. Alford, *Principles of Industrial Management*. New York: Ronald Press, 1947. This course helped create Japan's post-World War II industrial management system, and also may have had a role in the development of Lean management. See http://honoringhomer.net/ and http://deming.ces.clemson.edu/pub /den/giants_sarasohn.htm. See also W. Tsutsui, *Manufacturing Ideology: Scientific Management in Twentieth-Century Japan*, Princeton University press, Princeton New Jersey, 1998.

[4] We would need to gently get across the idea that a zero-sum management, stuffed with shortcuts, is entry-level, amateur management. In contrast, non-zero-sum management is for management professionals. A hallmark of professionalism is doing things that few other people can do. Anyone can do zero-sum management, of course. We should also try to get this same point across to business school deans and faculty, because their stock-in-trade has long been zero-sum management – even at the most highly regarded business schools.

[5] Frederick Taylor said: "… high speed… is the leading characteristic of good management." F. W. Taylor, *Shop Management*, Harper and Brothers Publishes, New York, NY, p. 77

[6] B. Emiliani, *Practical Lean Leadership: A Strategic Leadership Guide for Executives*, The CLBM, LLC, Wethersfield, Conn., 2008

## Chapter 8

[1] Lean management strengthens individuality through the correct application of the "Respect for People" principle, and also promotes more effective teamwork. Balance between the two is very important.

[2] Taiichi Ohno said: "A championship team combines good teamwork with individual skill." T. Ohno, *Toyota Production System: Beyond Large-Scale Production*, Productivity Press, Portland, OR, 1988, p. 8. Like so many things in the Toyota Way, it is important to achieve balance.

[3] See also J. Liker and M. Hoseus, *Toyota Culture*, McGraw-Hill, New York, NY, 2008, pp. 22-25

[4] Medical students learn many things, but one thing in particular is drilled into their head: Do no harm. Law students learn: Everyone has a right to representation. Engineering students learn: Use your technical education to ethically enhance humanity. What do business students learn? Maximize shareholder value? That's a shortcut.

[5] Maybe someone will re-discover the Lean management system 100 years from now.

[6] A recent study has shown that the highest-scoring traits of successful CEOs are: persistence, attention to detail, efficiency, analytical skills, and setting high standards. The lowest scoring traits of successful CEOs are: strong oral communication, teamwork, flexibility/adaptability, enthusiasm, and listening skills. Current state value stream maps which depict batch-and-queue processing (and thus approved by these successful CEOs) contradict the study's findings with regard to the highest scoring traits: i.e. that CEOs are not persistent, do not have attention to detail, are inefficient, have poor analytical skills, and set low standards. These current state value stream maps, filled with waste, unevenness, and unreasonableness, support the study finding with regard to the lowest scoring traits: i.e. that CEOs' success is, indeed, less dependent on strong oral communication skills, teamwork, flexibility/adaptability, enthusiasm, and listening skills. See S. Kaplan, M. Klebanov, and M. Sorensen, "Which CEO Characteristics and Abilities Matter?," working paper, April 2007, http://webuser.bus.umich.edu/departments/busecon/research/Entrepreneurship%20Workshops/June/Speaker%20papers/KaplanKlebanovSorensenApril302007.pdf.

**Appendix I**

[1] "The Toyota Way 2001," Toyota Motor Corporation, internal document, Toyota City, Japan, April 2001

[2] F.W. Taylor, *The Principles of Scientific Management*, Harper & Brothers Publishers, New York, NY, 1911

[3] W. Tsutsui, *Manufacturing Ideology: Scientific Management in Twentieth-Century Japan*, Princeton University Press, Princeton New Jersey, 1998

[4] R. Whatley Cooke-Taylor, *Modern Factory System*, Kegan Paul, Trench, Trubner & Co., Ltd., London, 1891, pp. 459-461

[5] F.W. Taylor, "Shop Management," *Transactions of The American Society of Mechanical Engineers*, Vol. 25, 1903, pp. 1337-1480

[6] H.S. Person, "Leadership in Scientific Management" in *Scientific Management in American Industry*, The Taylor Society, Harper and Brothers Publishers, New York, NY, 1929, pp. 427-439

[7] For more on understanding the "Respect for People" principle and its literal translation from Japanese, see the blog posting "Exploring the 'Respect for People' Principle of the Toyota Way" by Jon Miller dated 4 February 2008, http://www.gembapantarei.com/2008/02/exploring_the_respect_for_people_principle_of_the.html. See also Y. Sugimori, K. Kusunoki, F. Cho, and S. Uchikawa, "Toyota Production System and Kanban System Materialization

of Just-in-Time and Respect-for-Human System," *International Journal of Production Research*, Vol. 15, No. 6, 1977, pp. 553-564

[8] Toyota Motor Corporation, "Sustainability Report 2007," p. 57, http://www.toyota.co.jp/en/environmental_rep/07/download/index.html

[9] J.P. Womack, "Respect for People," e-mail to the Lean community, 20 December 2007, www.lean.org

[10] Toyota Motor Corporation, "Guiding Principles" http://www.toyota.co.jp/en/vision/philosophy/index.html and "Contribution Towards Sustainable Development" http://www.toyota.co.jp/en/vision/sustainability/index.html

[11] M.L. Emiliani, "Lean Behaviors," *Management Decision*, Vol. 36, No. 9, pp. 615-631, 1998

[12] F. W. Taylor, *Scientific Management: Comprising Shop Management, Principles of Scientific Management, Testimony Before the House Committee*, foreword by Harlow S. Person, Harper & Brothers Publishers, New York, NY, 1947

[13] S. Kamiya, *My Life With Toyota*, Toyota Motor Sales Co., Ltd., 1976, pp. 31, 48

[14] Y. Sugimori, K. Kusunoki, F. Cho, and S. Uchikawa, "Toyota Production System and Kanban System Materialization of Just-in-Time and Respect-for-Human System," *International Journal of Production Research*, Vol. 15, No. 6, 1977, pp. 553-564

[15] S. Kato, *My Years with Toyota*, Toyota Motor Sales Co., Ltd., 1981, p. 101

[16] Y. Monden, *Toyota Production System: Practical Approach to Production Management*, Industrial Engineering and Management Press, Norcross, GA, 1983, p. 11 and 141

[17] T. Ohno, *Toyota Production System: Beyond Large-Scale Production*, Productivity Press, Portland, OR, 1988, p. xiii

[18] M. Imai, *Kaizen: The Key to Japan's Competitive Success*, McGraw-Hill, New York, NY, 1987

[19] M. Imai, "Introduction to Kaizen," Kaizen Institute of America seminar at The Hartford Graduate Center, Hartford, Conn., May 9, 1988

[20] M. Husar, "Corporate Culture: Toyota's Secret, Competitive Advantage," General Motors internal paper, 16 May 1991, pp. 10-11

[21]. Y. Togo, *Yuki Togo's Sell Like Hell!!*, self-published, 1997, pp. 141-142

[22] J. Womack, D. Jones, and D. Roos, *The Machine that Changed the World*, Rawson Associates, New York, NY, 1990, Chapter 6

[23] T. Nishiguchi, *Strategic Industrial Sourcing*, Oxford University Press,

New York, NY, 1994

[24] T. Fujimoto, *The Evolution of a Manufacturing System at Toyota*, Oxford University Press, Inc., New York, NY, 1999

[25] J. Dyer and K. Nobeoka, "Creating and Managing a High Performance Knowledge-Sharing Network: The Toyota Case," *Strategic Management Journal*, Vol. 21, No. 3, 2000, pp. 345-367

[26] J. Liker and T. Choi, "Building Deep Supplier Relationships," *Harvard Business Review*, December 2004, pp. 104-113

[27] B. Emiliani, with D. Stec, L. Grasso, and J. Stodder, *Better Thinking, Better Results: Case Study and Analysis of an Enterprise-Wide Lean Transformation*, second edition, The CLBM, LLC, Wethersfield, Conn., 2007

[28] B. Emiliani, *REAL LEAN: Understanding the Lean Management System*, Volume One, The CLBM, LLC, Wethersfield, Conn., 2007

[29] B. Emiliani, *REAL LEAN: Critical Issues and Opportunities in Lean Management*, Volume Two, The CLBM, LLC, Wethersfield, Conn., 2007

[30] For a list of key papers, see www.theclbm.com

[31] B. Emiliani, *Practical Lean Leadership: A Strategic Leadership Guide for Executives*, The CLBM, LLC, Wethersfield, Conn., 2008

**Appendix II**

[1] Caux Round Table *Principles for Business*, 1994, http://www.cauxround-table.org/principles.html. Looking at these principles from another direction, they are an excellent resource for informing executives of the most likely areas in which they will stumble.

## Appendix I

### The Equally Important "Respect for People" Principle

*Lean community leaders have recently made two huge changes in how they present Lean. The first change is Lean as a management system rather than "Lean manufacturing." Second, they are finally taking note of the long-established "Respect for People" principle. Why now? In part because there have been so few successful Lean transformations over the last 20 years. Another reason is that most other aspects of the Lean management system have been studied in detail, so this is the next territory to explore. This batch-and-queue non-integrative approach has severely increased the lead-time needed to properly educatepeople about Lean management – particularly the "Respect for People" principle.*

The "Respect for People" principle is one of two pillars of The Toyota Way [1]; the other is "Continuous Improvement." The "Respect for People" principle has existed for several decades within Toyota's management system, but has been almost entirely ignored by outsiders. In addition, this principle extends back to the 1900s and was recognized as essential by the creators of the Scientific Management system [2] – of which Lean management is its direct descendent [3] in tandem with Ford's flow production system. In the old days, the "Respect for People" principle was referred to more narrowly as "Cooperation," principally between management and labor [4, 5].

As many people have found out firsthand, practicing only the "Continuous Improvement" principle (called "Betterment" in the old days [2, 5]) leads to many problems. Foremost among them is management's desire to improve efficiency and productivity usually results in layoffs, which slows down or halts improvement efforts. Root cause analyses of the problems that arise when only the "Continuous Improvement" principle is practiced indicates a countermeasure that today we call the "Respect for People" principle [3]. This point is worth repeating: "Respect for People" (Cooperation) is the primary countermeasure for bungled continuous improvement (Betterment) efforts. That's why it is a Toyota Way principle.

Indeed, the failure of the Scientific Management system to firmly establish itself in industry 60-100 years ago was correctly attributed to management's inability to establish long-term patterns of cooperative and respectful behavior with labor, in addition to other leadership shortcomings [6]. The same thing is happening today. Lean management is struggling to replace conventional management on a narrow basis, let alone across wide swaths of manufacturing and service industries. It should be no surprise that history is repeating itself.

The "Respect for People" principle is deceptive in that it seems very easy to understand and apply, but it is not. Most mid- and senior-level managers think they know what "Respect for People" means, but it is clear from leadership behaviors, common business performance metrics, company policies, management's decisions, and sometimes even corporate strategy, that they do not.

Top managers typically possess superficial, casual definitions of "Respect for People" such as fairness, civility, or listening. And they think they do these things quite well. Further, they think understanding the meaning of "Respect for People" is trivial for well-educated persons in high positions. This is a severe misjudgment. Far from being trivial, it is of great importance to the long-term survival and prosperity of a business to understand what "Respect for People" really means.

Toyota does not use one simple, discrete definition to express the "Respect for People" principle. Its context is better represented by the phrase "Respect for Stakeholders" in a narrow context [1] and also humanity in a larger context [7]. Rather, it is a more elaborate multi-layered description that includes historical words from former Toyota executives to better comprehend its meaning. Toyota's top-level representation of the "Respect for People" principle consists of two parts: "Respect" and "Teamwork," and is as follows [1, 8]:

> "RESPECT: We respect others, make every effort to understand each other, take responsibility and do our best to build mutual trust.

> TEAMWORK: We stimulate personal and professional growth, share the opportunities of development and maximize individual and team performance."

These words do not constitute the entire definition. A significant amount of detail is missing and can be found only in the "The Toyota Way 2001" document [1], which is not publicly available. But don't fall into the trap of hoping to obtain a copy of the document. Instead, please start to think about what "Respect for People" means in the context of stakeholders, corporate policies, metrics, business processes, leadership behaviors, corporate strategy, etc.

While the Toyota Way 2001 document does much to reduce variation in individual perceptions of what the equally important "Continuous Improvement" and "Respect for People" principles mean, words printed on paper are never sufficient. The "Respect for People" principle is comprehended only through daily thinking and practice on-the-job. It requires years of thought and practice to understand it well, and can never be completely comprehended.

James Womack, founder and chairman of the Lean Enterprise Institute, recently sent an e-mail note to the Lean community titled "Respect for People" [9]. In it he spoke of this principle in the context of the manager-associate dyad, which is what most people think of when they hear about the "Respect for People" principle. While this is a very important dyad, it is not the only relationship that matters.

The "Respect for People" principle encompasses all key stakeholders: employees, suppliers, customers, investors, and communities [1, 10]. Thus, rather than representing a single dyad, the "Respect for People" principle is a multilateral expression of the need for balanced, mutually respectful relationships, cooperation, and co-prosperity with these key stakeholders. So in the context of Lean management, the "Respect for People" principle is anything but trivial to understand.

It is worthwhile now to briefly trace the origins and evolution of this principle to illustrate that it has been around for many decades, but only rarely has it been put into effective practice by senior managers. That's because their focus has long been the near-singular pursuit of productivity and efficiency improvements to lower costs and increase profits, usually culminating in layoffs – a zero-sum outcome for employees that violates the "Respect for People" principle.

In the late 1800s, leading business thinkers and doers began to press for improved cooperation between labor and management to overcome systemic strife between these two parties. They did this for practical reasons, not theoretical ones. Poor cooperation increased costs, and these costs could be avoided. Today we would say: leadership behaviors that foment conflict are waste because they add cost but do not add value and can be eliminated [11].

R.W. Cooke-Taylor, the author of *Modern Factory System* [4] published in 1891, said:

> "Among reflections recently made was the disappointing one of the strained relations often existing under the modern factory system between employers and employed. Some grave dangers were pointed out which the future may have in store for us in this connection, and the inconveniences of the situation must be patent to everyone. The cure most usually proposed… is that of co-operation."

In this quote, "co-operation" means a business is operated jointly by labor and management, as "part proprietors," with profit-sharing, to "ameliorate the rivalries of capital and labor… [which] affects large savings in the cost of production."

In other words, eliminating wasteful labor-management rivalries reduces costs. However, we must not forget that wasteful rivalries can exist among other stakeholders such as suppliers, investors, and even customers, which also increase costs.

Soon thereafter "cooperation" took on a meaning in business that we are more familiar with: working together to satisfy common interests. In his 1903 paper titled "Shop Management," Frederick Taylor stressed the importance of cooperation and respect for people in the following ways [5]:

> "First, then, the men must be brought to see that the new system changes their employers from antagonists to friends who are working as hard as possible, side by side with them, all pushing in the same direction..."

> "In making this decision [to reorganize], as in taking each subsequent step, the most important consideration, which should always be first in the mind of the reformer, is 'what effect will this step have upon the workman'?"

> "The mistake that ninety-nine men [managers] out of a hundred make is that they have attempted to influence a large body of men at once [with major changes in the management system] instead of taking one man at a time."

The last quote is interesting because most senior managers today, just as they did in the early 1900s, impose change upon people in large batches, rather than one at a time. The latter approach recognizes employees as individuals whose concerns about changes in the management system are not uniform and can only be addressed by personal contact.

Frederick Taylor continued to stress the importance of cooperation and respect for people in his 1911 book, *The Principles of Scientific Management* [2]:

> "...almost every act of the workman should be preceded by one or more preparatory acts of the management which enable him to do his work better and quicker than he otherwise could."

> "They [management] heartily cooperate with the men so as to ensure all of the work is being done in accordance with the principles of the science which has been developed."

Taylor's most thorough explanation of the need for cooperation and respect for people is found in his testimony to Congress in 1912 [12].

That's the early view of cooperation and respect for people, which was seen as a practical necessity to reduce conflict and help achieve higher productivity, lower costs, and better quality.

So how could Lean practitioners have become familiar with the "Respect for People" principle prior to it coming to the forefront within the last few years? Well, it was hiding in plain view for decades; they would have found it to be a consistent theme in the writings and speeches of current and former Toyota executives, as well as some who have closely studied Toyota's management system. What follows are a few brief examples of where the "Respect for People" principle has appeared in various books and papers, arranged chronologically.

Shotaro Kamiya (d. 1980) was a past Chairman of Toyota Motor Sales. In his 1976 memoir *My Life With Toyota*, Kamiya refers to the "Respect for People" principle in terms of how automobile dealers are treated by automobile manufacturers [13] when he worked for General Motors (before joining Toyota, circa 1935):

> "Their [General Motors] policy toward dealers was especially merciless, and almost daily they cut ties with dealers in financial trouble. I remember thinking that while such action might be accepted business practice in the United States, where companies rely greatly on written contracts, customs are different in Japan and GM officers should try to understand the local situation more. I often complained to the American staff and tried to persuade them to help dealers instead of dropping them, especially since I visited dealers and knew firsthand their predicament. But GM ignored my complaints. It was at this time that I thought out one of my most important business principles, the necessity for coexistence and co-prosperity with dealers... my emphasis on respect for the dealer inspired many men from other companies to join Toyota."

Fujio Cho, the current Chairman of Toyota Motor Corporation, co-authored a paper in 1977 titled: "Toyota Production System and Kanban System: Materialization of Just-in-Time and Respect-for-Human System" [14]. The

"Respect for Human" system was characterized as follows:

> "...the 'respect-for-human' system where the workers
> are allowed to display in full their capabilities through
> active participation in running and improving their
> own workshops... which is the most distinctive fea-
> ture of Toyota's respect for human system."

> "Toyota firmly believes that making up a system
> where the capable Japanese workers can actively par-
> ticipate in running and improving their workshops and
> be able to fully display their capabilities would be
> [the] foundation of human respect environment of the
> highest order."

Toyota has profit sharing and associates who participate in operating the business. This sounds a lot like what R.W. Cook-Taylor said about "co-operation" in his 1891 book *Modern Factory System.* Here is another instructive quote from Mr. Cho's paper:

> "It is not a conveyer that operates men, while it is
> men that operate a conveyer, which is the first step to
> respect for human independence."

One could say today: "It is not a computer [e.g. SAP] that operates men, while it is men that operate a computer, which is the first step to respect for human independence."

Seisi Kato, who followed Shotaro Kamiya as Chairman of Toyota Motor Sales, said the following in his 1981 memoir, *My Years With Toyota* [15], in relation to employees and dealers:

"I adopted what I call the Three C's, standing for Communication, Consideration and Cooperation. What they signify is both a method of personal communication and a method of management. Handing down orders is not leadership, nor is issuing policies enough to constitute business relationships. In my view leadership is a process springing from dialogue that reaches the level of true communication, followed by sincere efforts at cooperation based upon mutual consideration and understanding of each other's position."

Professor Yasuhiro Monden's 1983 book *Toyota Production System: Practical Approach to Production Management*, states [16]:

"…respect-for-humanity, [which allows] each worker to participate in the production process."

"Respect for humanity: Since quality control based on autonomation calls immediate attention to defects or problems in the production process, it stimulates improvement activities and thus increases respect for humanity."

Taiichi Ohno, former Executive Vice President of Toyota Motor Corporation, said in the Preface of his 1988 book *Toyota Production System: Beyond Large-Scale Production* [17]:

"The most important objective of the Toyota System has been to increase production efficiency by consistently and thoroughly eliminating waste. This concept and the equally important respect for humanity that has passed down from the venerable Toyoda Sakichi (1867-1930), founder of the company and master of inventions, to his son Toyoda Kiichiro (1894-1952), Toyota Motor Company's first president and father of the Japanese passenger car, are the foundations of the Toyota production system."

Note the words "equally important," which means the "Respect for People" principle is not optional, though most mangers seem to think it is optional. And note that "eliminating waste" (continuous improvement) and "respect for humanity" are "the foundations" of Toyota's production system – and Toyota's overall management system as well. Too bad many people don't bother reading the Preface of books, or when they do read these books they are too focused on Lean tools to notice the foundational principles.

Masaaki Imai, founder and chairman of the Kaizen Institute, made significant efforts to reinforce respect for people, cooperation, etc., in his 1987 book, *Kaizen: The Key to Japan's Competitive Success* [18], and in his popular late-1980s kaizen training seminars [19].

In 1991 Michael Husar, who was an assembly coordinator at NUMMI, the General Motors-Toyota joint venture in Fremont, Calif., wrote an internal company paper titled: "Corporate Culture: Toyota's Secret, Competitive Advantage" [20]. The paper presented in a very concise and efficient way the differences between GM and Toyota corporate culture. It was intended for GM management, who was Husar's employer at the joint venture, as a way to help promote needed changes in GM's corporate culture.

The paper, based largely on Toyota internal training (similar in many ways to "The Toyota Way 2001" document that appeared 10 years later), contained a section titled: "Respect for the Value of People." In it, Husar says:

> "Toyota believes its growth as a business enterprise comes through the growth of its people. This means to be successful, Toyota must utilize its employees' abilities as effectively as possible, and help each person develop the ability to think and execute the job more effectively.

> Toyota has plants, equipment, and capital resources, but these things do not build cars. Its team members build the cars. Its team members also add value to its products by suggesting ways to improve their work and the production process. Toyota realizes that it is responsible for providing its employees the opportunity to contribute their ideas, as well as their labor.

> Toyota also believes that to get the best from its employees, it must respect their competence, and provide them with jobs that use and challenge their abilities. Toyota realizes the value of its people, and wants them to think of the company as a place where everyone can learn from one another, and grow as individuals, rather than just as a place to work."

Another section titled "Mutual Trust Between Employees and Management" says:

> "Mutual trust means that management and the

employees have confidence in one another. anagement and their employees have different jobs and different responsibilities in the company. Mutual trust comes from the belief that everyone is, however, striving for the same purpose...

Toyota realizes this kind of mutual trust is not a given condition between management and the employees. It must be earned through many mutual efforts that create confidence.

Toyota values and tries to maintain mutual trust, because it is the foundation for the growth of the company and its employees."

Yukiyasu Togo, another former Chairman of Toyota Motor Sales said in his 1997 memoir *Yuki Togo's Sell Like Hell!!* [21]:

"For two people to develop trustworthy and respectful relationships they must meet each other face to face as often as possible. This makes possible the very best opportunity for good communications. They must also show consideration of one another's situation, feelings, and needs, and share a willingness to cooperate... Without good human relations, you cannot really grow or prosper, so the 'Three C's' are a vital part of any success formula."

In the award-winning 1998 paper, "Lean Behaviors," I coined the terms "Lean behaviors" and "behavioral waste" [11]. The paper identifies value-added leadership behaviors (respect is one of them) and leadership behaviors that are waste because they add cost but do not value and can be eliminated. It says:

> "The concept of 'lean' behaviors is analogous to lean production. Lean behaviors are defined simply as behaviors that add or create value. It is the minimization of waste associated with arbitrary or contradictory thoughts and actions that leads to defensive behavior, ineffective relationships, poor cooperation, and negative attitudes.

> In contrast, behaviors that inhibit work flow are analogous to wasteful batch and queue mass production methods. These behaviors are... defined as behaviors that add no value and can be eliminated. They include the display of irrational and confusing information that results in delays or work stoppages, or the articulation of unsubstantiated subjective thoughts and opinions.

> It is not inconceivable that someday investors, suppliers, customers, or employees will begin to question the cost or ethics of 'fat' behaviors in a manner similar to recent stakeholder concerns about a company's environmental record or their presence in countries that lack basic human rights. Critical stakeholders such as investors or employees may precipitate improved behaviors once they more fully comprehend its impact on financial performance or quality of everyday life in the workplace. No stakeholder, except for competitors, would be happy if they knew the costs added to the goods or services that they purchase due to 'fat' behaviors."

The paper showed the tremendous amount of behavioral waste that leaders normally exhibit and how it undercuts respect and other value-added behaviors, which are absolutely required to make the Lean management system work. The "Respect for People" principle is not optional.

The 2003 Shingo Prize winning book *Better Thinking, Better Results: Case Study and Analysis of an Enterprise-Wide Lean Transformation* helped answer the question: "How do you conduct a Lean transformation?" It was a detailed case study and analysis of The Wiremold Company's enterprise-wide Lean transformation from 1991-2001. It presented Lean as a management system and was the first book to describe the application and integration of the "Continuous Improvement" and "Respect for People" principles in a business not affiliated with Toyota or its key suppliers.

Finally, the "Respect for People" principle has long existed in Toyota Motor Corporation's relationship with its customers through its "customer-first" rule [1, 13]. The "Respect for People" principle also exists in Toyota's relationship with its key suppliers, where the focus since 1939 has been joint problem solving and capability-building instead of bargaining over prices, long-term relationships, and co-prosperity. The results of this policy, introduced by Kiichiro Toyoda, the first president of Toyota Motor Corporation, are truly remarkable and have been extensively documented in recent years [22-26]. In addition, investors and communities have long been treated with respect and experienced mutual prosperity. This illustrates the broader intent and meaning of the "Respect for People" principle, which should really be understood as "Respect for Stakeholders" [1].

So there you have it; a quick tour of the origins and evolution of the "Respect for People" principle, and some of the books and papers in which it has appeared over time. This principle has been a consistent theme in Toyota's management thinking and practice – and before that also in the thinking and practice of Scientific Management.

Unfortunately, not only have most senior managers been unaware of, or, ignored the "Respect for People" principles for decades, but almost the entire Lean community outside of Toyota Motor Corporation has done so as well. Ignoring or failing to apply this fundamental principle over that last 30 years has surely held back the sincere efforts of both Lean advocates and Lean practitioners.

Jim Womack's e-mail note closed with a challenge:

> "The challenge for those of us in the Lean community is to embrace and explain the true nature of mutual respect for people – managers and associates...."

Womack's statement is supported by advocates of both Lean management and Scientific Management. After all, it is the "Respect for People" principle that makes Lean management work.

However, we must enlarge the challenge. We must embrace and explain how the "Respect for People" principle is a required part of the Lean management system, and that it extends beyond the narrow manager-associate dyad to encompass other people: customers, suppliers, investors, and communities. We must help senior managers understand that the "Respect for People" principle is inclusive of all key stakeholders, and how they can consistently apply the principle both day-to-day and strategically and in combination with the "Continuous Improvement" principle.

The focus of my four books and over a dozen papers written in the last decade has been to present Lean as a management system, to illuminate the "Respect for People" principle, and to describe the interplay between the "Respect for People" and "Continuous Improvement" principles [27-30].

Business leaders who want to know more about how to bring the "Respect for People" principle to life will benefit from reading the new workbook, *Practical Lean Leadership: A Strategic Leadership Guide for Executives* [31]. But remember: words printed on paper can be very helpful but are never sufficient. The "Respect for People" and "Continuous Improvement" principles are comprehended only through daily thinking and practice on-the-job.

In closing, you will have a pretty good basic understanding of Lean management when you can articulate how the "Respect for People" principle relates to takt time, standardized work, 5 Whys, heijunka, jidoka, just-in-time, set-up reduction, kanban, poka-yoke, kaizen, and visual controls, for each of the following categories of people: employees, suppliers, customers, investors, and communities – for all of these 11 items in all five categories, not just for a couple of items in one or two categories.

The "Respect for People" principle is anything but trivial to understand.

**Appendix II – Caux Round Table** *Principles for Business* **(1994)**
Reprinted with permission of the Caux Round Table [1]

**Introduction**
The Caux Round Table believes that the world business community should play an important role in improving economic and social conditions. As a statement of aspirations, this document aims to express a world standard against which business behavior can be measured. We seek to begin a process that identifies shared values, reconciles differing values, and thereby develops a shared perspective on business behavior acceptable to and honored by all.

These principles are rooted in two basic ethical ideals: kyosei and human dignity. The Japanese concept of kyosei means living and working together for the common good enabling cooperation and mutual prosperity to coexist with healthy and fair competition. "Human dignity" refers to the sacredness or value of each person as an end, not simply as a mean to the fulfillment of others' purposes or even majority prescription.

The General Principles in Section 2 seek to clarify the spirit of kyosei and "human dignity," while the specific Stakeholder Principles in Section 3 are concerned with their practical application.

In its language and form, the document owes a substantial debt to The Minnesota Principles, a statement of business behavior developed by the Minnesota Center for Corporate Responsibility. The Center hosted and chaired the drafting committee, which included Japanese, European, and United

States representatives.

Business behavior can affect relationships among nations and the prosperity and well-being of us all. Business is often the first contact between nations and, by the way in which it causes social and economic changes, has a significant impact on the level of fear or confidence felt by people worldwide. Members of the Caux Round Table place their first emphasis on putting one's own house in order, and on seeking to establish what is right rather than who is right.

### Section 1. Preamble
The mobility of employment, capital, products and technology is making business increasingly global in its transactions and its effects.

Law and market forces are necessary but insufficient guides for conduct.

Responsibility for the policies and actions of business and respect for the dignity and interests of its stakeholders are fundamental.

Shared values, including a commitment to shared prosperity, are as important for a global community as for communities of smaller scale.

For these reasons, and because business can be a powerful agent of positive social change, we offer the following principles as a foundation for dialogue and action by business leaders in search of business responsibility. In so doing, we affirm the necessity for moral values in business decision making. Without them, stable business relationships and a sustainable world community are impossible.

## Section 2. General Principles

### Principle 1. The Responsibilities Of Businesses: *Beyond Shareholders toward Stakeholders*

The value of a business to society is the wealth and employment it creates and the marketable products and services it provides to consumers at a reasonable price commensurate with quality. To create such value, a business must maintain its own economic health and viability, but survival is not a sufficient goal.

Businesses have a role to play in improving the lives of all their customers, employees, and shareholders by sharing with them the wealth they have created. Suppliers and competitors as well should expect businesses to honor their obligations in a spirit of honesty and fairness. As responsible citizens of the local, national, regional and global communities in which they operate, businesses share a part in shaping the future of those communities.

### Principle 2. The Economic and Social Impact of Business: *Toward Innovation, Justice and World Community*

Businesses established in foreign countries to develop, produce or sell should also contribute to the social advancement of those countries by creating productive employment and helping to raise the purchasing power of their citizens. Businesses also should contribute to human rights, education, welfare, and vitalization of the countries in which they operate.

Businesses should contribute to economic and social development not only in the countries in which they operate, but also in the world community at large, through effective and prudent use of resources, free and fair competition, and emphasis upon innovation in technology, production methods, marketing and communications.

### Principle 3. Business Behavior: *Beyond the Letter of Law Toward a Spirit of Trust*

While accepting the legitimacy of trade secrets, businesses should recognize that sincerity, candor, truthfulness, the keeping of promises, and transparency contribute not only to their own credibility and stability but also to the smoothness and efficiency of business transactions, particularly on the international level.

### Principle 4. Respect for Rules

To avoid trade frictions and to promote freer trade, equal conditions for competition, and fair and equitable treatment for all participants, businesses should respect international and domestic rules. In addition, they should recognize that some behavior, although legal, may still have adverse consequences.

### Principle 5. Support for Multilateral Trade

Businesses should support the multilateral trade systems of the GATT/World Trade Organization and similar international agreements. They should cooperate in efforts to promote the progressive and judicious liberalization of trade and to relax those domestic measures that unreasonably hinder global commerce, while giving due respect to national policy objectives.

## Principle 6. Respect for the Environment
A business should protect and, where possible, improve the environment, promote sustainable development, and prevent the wasteful use of natural resources.

## Principle 7. Avoidance of Illicit Operations
A business should not participate in or condone bribery, money laundering, or other corrupt practices: indeed, it should seek cooperation with others to eliminate them. It should not trade in arms or other materials used for terrorist activities, drug traffic or other organized crime.

## Section 3. Stakeholder Principles

### Customers
We believe in treating all customers with dignity, irrespective of whether they purchase our products and services directly from us or otherwise acquire them in the market. We therefore have a responsibility to:

- provide our customers with the highest quality products and services consistent with their requirements;
- treat our customers fairly in all aspects of our business transactions, including a high level of service and remedies for their dissatisfaction;
- make every effort to ensure that the health and safety of our customers, as well as the quality of their environment, will be sustained or enhanced by our products and services;

- assure respect for human dignity in products offered, marketing, and advertising; and respect the integrity of the culture of our customers.

**Employees**
We believe in the dignity of every employee and in taking employee interests seriously. We therefore have a responsibility to:

- provide jobs and compensation that improve workers' living conditions;
- provide working conditions that respect each employee's health and dignity;
- be honest in communications with employees and open in sharing information, limited only by legal and competitive constraints;
- listen to and, where possible, act on employee suggestions, ideas, requests and complaints;
- engage in good faith negotiations when conflict arises;
- avoid discriminatory practices and guarantee equal treatment and opportunity in areas such as gender, age, race, and religion;
- promote in the business itself the employment of differently abled people in places of work where they can be genuinely useful;
- protect employees from avoidable injury and illness in the workplace;
- encourage and assist employees in developing relevant and transferable skills and knowledge; and
- be sensitive to the serious unemployment problems frequently associated with business decisions, and work with governments, employee groups, other agencies and each

other in addressing these dislocations.

## Owners / Investors

We believe in honoring the trust our investors place in us. We therefore have a responsibility to:

- apply professional and diligent management in order to secure a fair and competitive return on our owners' investment;
- disclose relevant information to owners/investors subject to legal requirements and competitive constraints;
- conserve, protect, and increase the owners/investors' assets; and
- respect owners/investors' requests, suggestions, complaints, and formal resolutions.

## Suppliers

Our relationship with suppliers and subcontractors must be based on mutual respect. We therefore have a responsibility to:

- seek fairness and truthfulness in all our activities, including pricing, licensing, and rights to sell;
- ensure that our business activities are free from coercion and unnecessary litigation;
- foster long-term stability in the supplier relationship in return for value, quality, competitiveness and reliability;
- share information with suppliers and integrate them into our planning processes;
- pay suppliers on time and in accordance with agreed terms of trade; and
- seek, encourage and prefer suppliers and subcontractors whose employment practices respect human dignity.

## Competitors

We believe that fair economic competition is one of the basic requirements for increasing the wealth of nations and ultimately for making possible the just distribution of goods and services. We therefore have a responsibility to:

- foster open markets for trade and investment;
- promote competitive behavior that is socially and environmentally beneficial and demonstrates mutual respect among competitors;
- refrain from either seeking or participating in questionable payments or favors to secure competitive advantages;
- respect both tangible and intellectual property rights; and
- refuse to acquire commercial information by dishonest or unethical means, such as industrial espionage.

## Communities

We believe that as global corporate citizens we can contribute to such forces of reform and human rights as are at work in the communities in which we operate. We therefore have a responsibility in those communities to:

- respect human rights and democratic institutions, and promote them wherever practicable;
- recognize government's legitimate obligation to the society at large and support public policies and practices that promote human development through harmonious relations between business and other segments of society;
- collaborate with those forces in the community dedicated to raising standards of health, education, workplace safety and economic well-being;
- promote and stimulate sustainable development and play a

leading role in preserving and enhancing the physical environment and conserving the earth's resources;
- support peace, security, diversity and social integration;
- respect the integrity of local cultures; and
- be a good corporate citizen through charitable donations, educational and cultural contributions, and employee participation in community and civic affairs.

## About the Author

 M.L. "Bob" Emiliani is a professor at Connecticut State University in New Britain, Conn., where he teaches various courses on Lean management.

He worked in the consumer products and aerospace industries for nearly two decades and held management positions in engineering, manufacturing, and supply chain management, and had responsibility for implementing Lean in manufacturing operations and supply chains.

Emiliani has authored or co-authored a dozen papers related to Lean leadership including: "Lean Behaviors" (1998), "Linking Leaders' Beliefs to their Behaviors and Competencies" (2003), "Using Value Stream Maps to Improve Leadership" (2004), "Origins of Lean Management in America: The Role of Connecticut Businesses" (2006), and "Standardized Work for Executive Leadership (2008). Five of his papers have won awards for excellence.

He is the principal author of the book *Better Thinking, Better Results: Case Study and Analysis of an Enterprise-Wide Lean Transformation*, (second edition, 2007), a detailed case study and analysis of The Wiremold Company's Lean transformation from 1991 to 2001. It won a Shingo Research Prize in 2003 as the first book to describe an enterprise-wide Lean transformation in a real company where both principles of Lean management – "Continuous Improvement" and "Respect for People" – were applied.

He is also the author of *REAL LEAN: Understanding the Lean Management System* (Volume One) and *REAL LEAN: Critical Issues and Opportunities in Lean Management* (Volume Two), both published in 2007, and *Practical Lean Leadership: A Strategic Leadership Guide For Executives*, published in 2008.

Emiliani holds engineering degrees from the University of Miami, the University of Rhode Island, and Brown University.

He is the owner of The Center for Lean Business Management, LLC. (www.theclbm.com).

"What waste is allowed by the master?"

- Charles Babbage, *On the Economy of Machinery and Manufactures*, 1832, p. 76

5S (Five S), vii

14 decision points, 98-100

*á la carte*, 35

accounting

    absorption (standard cost), 60, 64, 65

    education, 15

    methods, 31

    rules, 30

    system, 12, 14-15, 16

*ad hominem*, 114n

Alford, L., 117n

alloy(s), 68-71

    -ing, 70, 73, 96, 99

    iron-carbon, 68-70

arbitrary decisions, 54

assumptions, 10, 81-82

    canonical, 95-96

    incorrect (faulty), 6, 109

athletes, 23

audits, 96

authority, 5, 6, 37, 55, 71

autocracy

    corporate, 56, 96

autocrat, 55-56, 66

Babbage, Charles, 112n, 150

Bach, J.S., 46

backslide, 10, 11, 16, 17, 67

Baggaley, B., 102n, 106n, 112n

balance, 43, 45, 56, 70, 79, 117n, 124

Basu, S., 102n, 108n, 115n

batch-and-queue

    definition, 2-3

    thinking, 38

metrics, 14, 32

    processing, 12, 50, 59, 92, 110n

    production, 57, 66

Bedaux, Charles, 19-20, 21

Bedaux consultants, 19, 20, 21, 22, 23, 39

behavioral waste (8th waste), 133-135

behaviors, 3, 4, 78, 116n, 122, 123, 124, 125, 133

    obsequious, 15, 54

    opportunistic, 43, 75

    value-added, 135

benchmarks, 60

"Betterment," 122

bilateral, 84

Black, J., 113n

blame, ix, 6, 24, 26, 32, 92, 104n, 116n

blindness, 54, 111n

board(s) of directors, 6

books, v, 21, 22, 26, 34, 89, 90, 101n, 116n, 128, 131, 136, 137

bottom-up, 19

Brandenburg Concerto, 46

budget, 12, 15-16, 57, 108n

business, 1-3

    certainties, 12-13

    definition, 1

    metrics, 5, 12, 14, 15, 16, 32, 122, 124

    principles, 39-40, 47, 80-82, 96, 99, 128

    school, 40, 103n, 117n

buy-in, 5, 19, 21

buyers' market, 29, 57, 59, 61, 63,

76, 77, 104*n*
definition, 4-5
CEO, 10, 13, 14, 19, 22, 30, 41,
    67, 101*n*, 118*n*
    playbook, 35
    traits, 118*n*
CFO, 14, 15, 30
canonical assumptions, 95-96
capitalism, 66, 75, 77, 96, 114*n*
capitalists, 68, 70-71, 76, 113*n*
    free market, 68, 76, 114*n*
carbon, 68-70
carbon dioxide, 111*n*
cars, 79, 132
cash flow, 30
Caux Round Table *Principles for
    Business*, 41-43, 45, 46, 110*n*,
    120n, 139-147
central planning, 66, 113*n*
cheat(ing), 23, 32, 83
cherry-pick(ing), 20, 51-53, 99
Cho, Fujio, iv, 78, 80, 113*n*, 118*n*-
    119*n*, 128-129
Choi, T., 120*n*
chopstix, 43
CliffsNotes, 32
closed system, 35
complacency, 10, 54
confirmation bias, 33
conflict, 13, 96, 125, 127, 144
Congress, 30, 127
conserberal, 80
conservative, 51, 64, 67, 75, 78-80,
    113*n*, 114*n*
    fiscally, 65
    values, 96

consultants, 19-23, 37, 39, 43, 90-
    92, 97, 116*n*
continuous improvement, 10, 50
    83, 112*n*
"Continuous Improvement" princi-
    ple, 2, 9, 49, 54, 121-137
control, 5, 12, 27, 31, 37, 56, 65,
    71, 113n, 130, 137
controlled economy, 76
conventional management, vi, ix,
    11-12, 31, 49, 54-55, 67, 77, 97,
    101*n*, 122
    forces, 12
Cooke-Taylor, R.W., 108*n*, 118*n*,
    125, 129
cooperation, 85, 124, 130, 131,
    134
"Cooperation," 51, 121, 122, 125-
    127, 129
corporate
    autocracy, 56, 96
    democracy, 56
    microeconomic policy, 56, 59,
    63, 65, 66, 67, 70
    purpose, 55, 78-82, 96, 100,
    102*n*, 115*n*
corporation (the), 55, 71
cost
    accounting, 16, 60, 63, 64, 65
    -cutting expert, 107*n*, 108*n*
    increases, 43, 55, 60
    of conflict, 96
    problems, 19, 37, 113*n*
    reduction, 30
countermeasures, ix, 6, 10, 17, 26,
    93, 97, 110*n*
Cowley, M., 102*n*

create wealth, 29, 30, 35

crisis, 20, 35, 52

Crowther, S., 101*n*

Cunningham, J., 106*n*

customer

demand, 44, 57, 66

-focused, 5, 29

current state, 19, 107*n*

customer first, 135

cycling, 39

DNA, 10, 105*n*

Day, P., 115*n*

decision points, 6-7, 25, 27, 28, 36, 46, 47, 51, 53, 67, 73, 82, 87, 98-100

Declaration of Independence, 80

defective parts, 80-81

defective ideas, 81-82

defense, 55

delegate, 21

demand-side, 113*n*

microeconomics, 63, 64, 65, 67, 70, 99, 111*n*, 112*n*, 113*n*

policy, 63, 67, 70

democracy, 55, 72

corporate, 56

deoxyribonucleic acid, 10

do-loop, 33

dogma(tic), 72, 73, 98, 99

Dollar Tree, 112*n*

Domb, E., 102*n*

Dyer, J., 120*n*

earth, 11

economic freedom, 67, 96

eco nomics, 65

economics (micro), 75, 77, 92, 109*n*

demand-side, 63-65, 67, 70, 99, 111*n*, 112*n*, 113*n*

supply-side, 55, 59, 60, 63-67, 70, 71, 96, 99, 111*n*, 112*n*, 113*n*

economic man, 33, 55, 59, 60, 85, 96, 108*n*, 109*n*

economists, 33, 60, 63, 64, 66

ego clashes, 90

eight wastes, 4

Emiliani, M.L. "Bob," 101*n*, 102*n*, 104*n*, 105*n*, 106*n*, 109*n*, 110*n*, 111*n*, 116*n*, 117*n*, 119*n*, 120*n*, 148-149

Enron, 29, 79

enterprise value, 3, 35, 45

equation

determinate, 27

indeterminate, 27

errors, 6, 15, 21, 24, 26, 60, 81, 86, 95, 107*n*, 114*n*

unforced, 12, 14, 81

ethics, 92, 134, 108*n*, 117*n*

executive(s)

as autocrat, 55-56

as king, 24, 25

as teachers, 55

beliefs, ix, 49, 51, 55-56, 71, 72, 99

characterization (general), viii-ix

decision points, 6-7, 25, 27, 28, 36, 46, 47, 51, 53, 67, 73, 82, 87, 98-100

excuses, 85, 86, 116*n*

know it all, 26, 27, 60, 84-85, 96, 98, 107*n*, 113*n*

learning Lean, 115$n$-116$n$
participation (in Lean), 15-16
pay, 59
promotion, 107$n$
reading, 21, 26, 107$n$
resistance, 22, 49, 85
role, 5-6, 29
stumble, 110$n$, 120$n$
exercise, 106$n$
Fackler, M., 106$n$
fact-based, ix, 83, 86
fair(ness), 35, 54, 55, 56, 70, 72, 75, 78, 96, 123$n$
FAKE Lean, 9, 11, 14, 52, 60, 90, 104$n$,
    definition, 2
Family Dollar, 112$n$
fat behaviors, 134
Fernandez, L., 104$n$
firefighting, 23, 107$n$, 110$n$
fiscally
    conservative, 65
    irresponsible, 59, 67
    responsible, 63, 67
Fishman, C., 105$n$
Fiume, O., 106$n$
Five S (5S), vii
flavor-of-the-month, 91
flavors (of Lean), 25
flexible thinking, 72, 98
Florida, 53
flow, 44
    information, 92
    production, vii, 19, 63, 121
    work, 134

football, 55, 103$n$
Ford, Henry, vii, 19, 63-64, 101$n$, 104$n$
forecasts (fortune-telling), 32
Frank, R., 113$n$
free lunch, 33
free market, 68, 76, 114$n$
free pass, 33, 59
free riders, 75
freedom, 37
Fujimoto, T., 102$n$, 120$n$
future state, 91
gamblers, 30
game changers, 50
gamers, 30
Gantt, Henry, 23-24, 25, 26, 107$n$
Gapper, J., 115$n$
General Motors, 55, 103$n$, 113$n$, 119$n$, 128, 131
getting even, 55, 75
Golden Rule, 75
golfers, 91
gradualism, 50
Grasso, L., 101$n$, 102$n$, 105$n$, 106$n$, 109$n$, 120$n$
gravity, 11-12
Hammond, J., 109$n$
hard-wired, 34, 114$n$
harmony, 79, 96, 115$n$
Hino, S., 102$n$
home run(s), 50, 97
Hoseus, M., 102$n$, 104$n$, 105$n$, 117$n$
hot-button issues, 55, 96
House Committee (investigating the Taylor System), vi

human programming, 34
Huntzinger, J., 106*n*, 112*n*, 115*n*
Husar, M., 119*n*, 131-132
ideology, 98
ideologue, 64, 72
ignore
   costs, 33
   facts, 86
   problems, 98
   "Respect for People," 136
ikusei (nurturing), 105*n*
Imai, M., 119*n*, 131
individual rights, 96
individual skill, 117*n*
individualism, 53, 54
individuality, 96, 117*n*
industrial management course,
   116*n*-117*n*
information (infonomics), 92
injustice, 75
Ingram, J.K., 108*n*-109*n*
insider trading, 32
inventory, 4
   finished goods, 65, 113*n*
   turns, 64, 70, 112*n*-113*n*
   work-in-process, 65, 113*n*
   zero, 66-67
investor(s), 43, 47, 96, 99
iron, 68-70
Jacoby, S., 115*n*
Japan, 75-76, 116*n*-117*n*, 128, 131
Jones, D., 119*n*
justice, 55, 56, 72
kaizen, 54, 56, 116*n*, 131, 137
   definition, 4

Kamiya, S., 119*n*, 128, 129
Kaplan, S., 118*n*
Kato, S., 119*n*, 129-130
Keeney, R., 109*n*
Kimball, D., 116*n*-117*n*
king, 24, 25
kitten (Grace the seal point
   Himalayan, at 6 weeks), 52
Klebanov, M., 118*n*
know it all, 26, 27, 60, 85, 96, 98,
   107*n*, 113*n*
Kusunoki, K., 118*n*-119*n*
labels, 68
labor, 39, 121, 122, 125-126, 132
   costs, 110*n*
   division of, 37
   market, 37
   wages, 110*n*
   union, 31
*laissez faire*, 66, 113*n*-114*n*
Lamoreaux, N., 106*n*
layoff(s), 31, 32, 37, 122, 125
Lean
   accounting, 14, 15, 63, 102*n*,
   111*n*
   as a "manufacturing thing," vii,
   52
   as a threat, ix, 49, 51, 53
   as an "initiative," 52
   asking executives to do, 53
   behaviors, 133-134
   culture, 9-10, 102*n*, 104-105*n*,
   FAKE, 2, 9, 11, 14, 52, 60, 90,
   104*n*
   journey, 10, 101*n*
   leader, 35, 107*n*

metrics, 14-15
misapply, 12, 14, 16
mischaracterized, vii, 49, 90
misunderstand, 12-13, 16, 49, 90
misuse, 51
  principles, v, 2, 9, 14, 51, 54,
  116*n*
  steals knowledge, 53-54
  sustainability, viii, ix, 9-10, 12,
  92, 105*n*, 106*n*
  sustaining, viii-ix, 6, 7, 9, 12,
  15, 16, 17, 49, 65, 68, 98-100
  tools, vii, 14, 13122
Lean enterprise
  estate planning, 17
Lean Enterprise Institute, 90, 104*n*,
  111*n*, 124
Lean management, ubiquitous
  books, 101*n*-102*n*
  definition, 1
  learning, 115*n*-116*n*
  low-fidelity, 25, 92
  movement, 9, 89-93
  principles, 2
Lean movement
  similarities to Scientific
  Management, 90
  sustaining, 89-93
leadership, 111*n*
  behaviors, 3, 4, 122, 124, 125,
  133
  definition, 3
  servant, 25, 55, 98
  time, 115*n*-116*n*
level loading, 50
liberal(s), 67, 68, 78-80, 114*n*

policy, 67
Liker, J., 102*n*, 104*n*, 105*n*, 115*n*,
  117*n*, 120*n*
litigation, 43
loafing, 53, 54
Lohr, S., 114*n*
long-term, 1, 2, 20, 23, 45, 46, 78,
  98, 103*n*, 110*n*, 123, 135
long-wave current state, xi, 17, 19-
  28, 75, 89
lottery, 32
low-fidelity, 25, 92
lunatic fringe, 35
MBA, 31
MRP, 66
managers
  as teachers, 55, 85, 96
Mann, D., 102*n* 104*n*
Maskell, B., 102*n*, 106*n*, 111*n*,
  112*n*
Mason, R., 111*n*
material, 39, 70, 77, 85, 112*n*
maximize shareholder value, 29,
  79, 96, 117*n*
McInerny, D., 114*n*
Meier, D., 102*n*, 115*n*
mental rigidity, 72
metallurgist, 26
metrics, 5, 12, 14, 15, 16, 32, 122,
  124
  batch-and-queue, 14, 31
  Lean, 14-15
microeconomic, 75, 96
  classical, 33, 59, 60, 63, 66
  neo-classical, 33, 59, 60, 63, 66
  policy, 56, 59, 63-67, 70, 111*n*,

112*n*

policy, state-run, 66

microeconomics, 55, 59-60, 63-67, 70-71, 96, 99, 111*n*

mid-term, 23

Mill, J.S., 108*n*

Miller, J., 103*n*, 118*n*

Minoura, T., 105*n*, 113*n*

Mito, S., 114*n*

Moffett, S., 106*n*

Monden, Y., 102*n*, 119*n*, 130

monopoly, 57, 61, 76

multilateral, 4, 40, 46, 47, 85, 99, 124

music, 23, 43-44, 46, 53, 85, 95, 115*n*-116*n*

practice, 85

musicians, 23, 46, 95

mutual respect, x, 96, 136

mutual trust, x, 123, 132-133

NIST/MEP, 90

NUMMI, 131

Nelson, D., 106*n*

Nishiguchi, T., 119*n*-120*n*

Nobeoka, K., 120*n*

non-zero-sum, 1, 27-28, 35, 40-41, 45, 46, 47, 49, 54, 75, 81, 97, 98, 99, 103*n*, 117*n*

definition, 1

obsessive-compulsive behavior, 34

Ocean State Job Lot, 112*n*

oddballs, 35

offense, 55

Ohno, Taiichi, 66-67, 72, 76-77, 95, 101*n*, 102*n*, 104*n*, 113*n*, 114*n*, 117*n*, 119*n*, 130-131

one best way, 50

open system, 35

operations, 20, 51

orbit, 11-12

outsource, 21, 31

overhead, 39

overproduce, 59

overproduction, 4, 31, 57, 59, 60, 63, 64, 66, 112*n*, 113*n*

overstock.com, 112*n*

ownership (company), 12-13, 16, 55, 71, 91

Palmer, A., 104*n*

pearlite eutectoid, 69, 70

people
are the problem, 50

Person, Harlow, vi, 101*n*, 118*n*, 119*n*

phase diagram, 68-70

physician, 26

piano, 43

planned economy, 66, 76, 77, 113*n*

player haters, 116*n*

politics, 3, 54, 55, 72, 96, 111*n*
organizational, 3, 54, 111*n*

power, 12, 37, 49, 56, 71, 84, 107*n*, 110*n*

price, 3, 33, 39, 43, 60, 103*n*, 135

price fixing, 32

prized possessions, 53

problems, vii, ix, x, 19, 22-23, 32-33, 37-47, 55, 67, 92, 93, 98, 99, 103*n*, 107*n*, 108*n*, 110*n*, 111*n*, 113n, 122, 130
algebraic view, 38
calculus view, 44

process and results, 92

productive capacity, 65

profit, 41, 42, 125
  -ability, 19, 20, 97
  sharing, 125, 129

progressives, 68

prosperity, 45, 60, 63, 98, 112*n*, 123, 124, 128, 135

Protzman, C., 116*n*

pull, 77

pull production (system), 61, 62, 63, 77

purpose (corporate), 55, 71, 78-82, 96, 97, 100, 115*n*

push production (system), 50, 63, 157

quick-hit(s), 31

radio, 53

Raff, D., 106*n*

Raiffa, H., 109*n*

Raman, A., 107*n*

rational self-interested maximizer, 33, 34, 59, 60, 66, 71

read(ing), 21, 26, 32, 107*n*, 108*n*, 131

REAL LEAN, x, 2, 9, 11, 14, 52, 60, 64, 72, 91, 95, 107*n*

reform(s), 67, 76, 78, 112*n*, 126

reform-minded, 78, 80

resistance (from executives), 22, 49, 85, 112*n*-113*n*

respect, 123

respect for humanity, 1, 103*n*, 123, 130-131

"Respect for People" principle, 2, 9, 14, 49, 50, 51, 54, 96, 101*n*, 103*n*-104*n*, 117*n*, 118*n*, 121-137

  equally important, 121-137
  relation to takt time, standardized work, etc., 137

respect for stakeholders, 123, 135

responsibility, 13, 24, 29, 55, 72, 83, 84, 123

reward(s), 29, 34, 39, 55, 57, 66, 71

risk, viii, 21, 65, 107*n*

Roos, D., 119n

root cause, ix, 6, 26, 93, 97, 107*n*, 110*n*, 122

Rother, M., 104*n*

Rowley, I., 115*n*

SAP (software), 129

salt, 71, 113*n*

Sarasohn, H., 116*n*-117*n*

satisfy(ing) customers, 29, 30, 75

Say, J-B., 111*n*-112*n*

Say's Law (conjecture), 111*n*-112*n*

Schonberger, R., 113*n*

school, 28, 32, 84, 85, 90, 97
  business, 40, 103*n*, 117*n*
  college, 31, 32, 90
  elementary, 40
  high, 32, 84, 90
  middle, 31, 90

Scientific Management, vi-viii, 13, 14, 19-22, 24, 25, 37, 39, 51, 63, 89, 90, 91, 97, 116*n*-117*n*, 121, 122, 127, 136
  failure, vi

scientific method, 1, 108*n*

scientist, 26

sects
  Lean, 90

Scientific Management, 90
self-check device, 80-81
self-interest, 56, 67, 85, 108*n*
self-serving, v, 25, 98
self-sufficiency, 55, 72
selfish(ness), 33, 53, 57, 59, 75, 82
sellers' market, 50, 57, 60, 64, 77
    definition, 4-5
servant leadership, 25, 55, 98
seven certainties, 16, 17
seven strikes, 16, 97
seven wastes, 63
sharing, 37, 50, 68, 70, 71, 75-82,
    96, 100
shareholder(s), 30, 50, 55, 103*n*
    -focused, 29
    value, 3, 35
Shingo Prize, 135
Shingo, S., 115*n*
Shirouzu, N., 105*n*, 106*n*
Shook, J., 104*n*
short-term
    assignments, 39
    focus, 22, 23, 34, 91
    gains, 14
    goals, 39
    needs, 22
    pressure, 34, 40
    problems, 22-23, 110*n*
    results, 23, 39, 91
    rewards, 39
    thinking, 32, 34, 39, 41-45, 110*n*
shortcut(s), 21, 23, 24, 25, 27, 29-
    36, 40, 41-47, 50, 51, 53, 67, 73,
    82, 86, 91, 96, 98-100, 108*n*,
    109*n*, 110*n*, 117*n*

definition, 1
legislative and regulatory, 30
    management, 31
Simons, D., 111*n*
Six Sigma, 51, 113*n*
Smith, Adam, 108*n*
social status, 55, 72
socialism, 75
socialist(s), 66, 68, 113*n*, 114*n*
sophistry, 84, 110*n*, 114*n*
Sorensen, M., 118*n*
soup, 71, 113*n*
sparknotes.com, 32
Spear, S., 106*n*
spices, 71
sprinters, 39
stakeholders, 41, 43, 45, 46, 47,
    49, 50, 54, 55, 56, 70, 71, 75,
    78, 80, 96, 98, 99, 103*n*, 124,
    126, 134, 137
    definition, 2
    marginalized, 43, 45, 55, 96
    respect for, 123, 135
stamping machine, 80
standard cost accounting, 60, 64,
    65-66
status symbols, 53-55, 72, 113*n*
Stec, D., 101*n*, 102*n*, 105*n*, 106*n*,
    109*n*, 111*n*, 120*n*
steel, 69-70
    composition, 69-70
    hardness, 69-70
    strength, 69-70
Stewart, T., 107*n*
stock option backdating, 32
Stodder, J., 101*n*, 102*n*, 105*n*,

106n, 109n, 120n

strategic planning, 102n

strategies and tactics, viii, 89, 91

strategy, 19, 21, 39, 91, 122, 124

students, 32, 83-87, 100
business, 117n
engineering, 117n
good characteristics, 83
law, 117n
medical, 117n
worst, 84

Sugimori, Y., 118n-119n

supply chain, 60

supply-side, 63, 65, 99, 113n
microeconomics, 55, 59, 60, 64-67, 70-71, 96, 111n, 112n, 113n
policy, 59, 67, 70

system, vi-ix, 1
definition, 2

TWI, 84

takt time, 50, 137

Taylor, A., 115n

Taylor, Frederick, vi, 23, 101n, 110n-111n, 117n, 118n, 119n, 126-127

Taylor Society, vi, 20, 90, 91

teacher(s), 40, 55, 83-85, 97

teamwork, 46, 54, 85-86, 116n, 117n, 123
undercutting, 116n

theory, 25, 81

Thornton, E., 109n

Three C's, 130

thunderstorm, 53

time (chronomics), 92,

time (to learn Lean), 115n-116n

Togo, Y., 119n, 133

top-down, ix, 5, 19

total cost, 112n

Toyoda, 76, 114n
Kiichiro, 75, 77, 114n, 131, 135
Precepts, 40, 46, 79-80, 110n, 115n
Sakichi, 131

Toyota, 64, 70, 72, 75, 97, 107n, 123, 127-135
Contribution Towards Sustainable Development, 40, 46, 79-80, 110n, 115n, 119n
corporate purpose, 78-80, 115n
customers, 135
DNA, 10, 105n, 106n
executives, 10, 16, 17, 40, 46, 72, 78-80, 97-98, 123, 127-131
Guiding Principles, 40, 46, 79-80, 110n, 115n, 119n
inventory turns, 64, 112n, 113n
investors, 135
management system, 16, 63, 72, 75, 102n, 131
mindset, 97, 102n
Motor Corporation, 10, 16, 27, 40, 75, 78, 97, 114n, 128, 130, 135, 136
production system, 67, 76-77, 105n, 118n, 119n, 128, 130, 131
suppliers, 135
Way, 10, 16, 27, 102n, 103n, 104n, 105n, 106n, 107n, 115n, 117n, 118n, 121-124, 132

training, 16, 28, 34, 39, 90, 105n, 113n, 114n, 116n, 131, 132

tricks, bag of, 29

trust, 56, 123, 132-133

Tsutsui, W., 101*n*, 117*n*, 118*n*

UFO, 35

U.S. Constitution, 79-80

Uchikawa, S., 118*n*-119*n*

ugly truths, 54

underproduction, 66

unforced errors, 12, 14, 81

unit cost, 112*n*

United States, 76, 112*n*, 128

unevenness, 35-36, 49, 50, 59, 63, 79, 85, 86, 92, 108*n*, 118*n*
  definition, 3

unreasonableness, 1, 35-36, 49, 50, 59, 63, 79, 85, 86, 92, 108*n*, 118*n*
  definition, 4

value
  definition, 3

value stream map(s), vii, 4, 56-63, 111*n*
  current state, 50, 54, 56-59, 65, 66, 110*n*, 118*n*
  future state, 61-63

Wada, K., 114*n*

wages, 30, 37, 110*n*

Wall Street, 34

*Wall Street Journal*, 108*n*

Washington gridlock, 112*n*

Watanabe, Katsuaki, 27

waste, 1, 4, 15, 35-36, 49, 50, 54, 56, 59, 63, 66, 79, 81, 85, 86, 92, 107*n*, 108*n*, 118*n*, 125, 130, 131, 133-135, 150
  definition, 3
  eight types, 4

wealth, 29-30, 33, 35, 37, 70, 75, 82, 100, 108*n*, 109*n*, 112*n*, 113*n*
  from waste, 35
  transfer, 35

Welch, D., 105*n*

welfare, 78

Wenner, N., 114*n*

Whitfield, K., 115*n*

Wiremold Company, 9, 35, 135

Womack, J.P., 101*n*, 105*n*, 119*n*, 124, 136

world-class, 23

World War II, vii, 75, 117*n*

Yui, T., 114*n*

zero-sum, 2-3, 12, 22, 25, 26, 27, 28, 31, 35, 41-45, 50, 51, 85, 86, 92, 96, 97, 102*n*-103*n*, 107*n*, 115n, 117*n*, 125
  definition, 1-2